C000265046

# W1̲N̲N̲E̲R̲S̲

## HORSES TO FOLLOW – FLAT 2024

Sixty-second year of publication

Contributors:
Rodney Pettinga
Richard Young

RACING POST

Commissioned by RACING POST, Floor 7, Vivo Building South Bank Central, 30 Stamford Street, London, SE1 9LS

First published in 2024 by PITCH PUBLISHING Ltd
9 Donnington Park, 85 Birdham Road, Chichester, West Sussex, PO20 7AJ
Order line: 01933 304 858

ISBN 9781839501456-

Printed and bound in Great Britain by Short Run Press Ltd

# 100 WINNERS

## HORSES TO FOLLOW – FLAT 2024

(ages as at 2024)

### ABSURDE (FR)

*6 b g Fastnet Rock - Incroyable (Singspiel)*

A dual winner over 1m2f for Carlos Laffon-Parias in his native France in 2021 and 2022, Absurde joined Willie Mullins in May last year and he ran out an impressive winner of a 2m4f novice hurdle at Killarney for his new trainer that month. That race was one he was entitled to win but, switched to the Flat in June, he very much caught the eye by finishing second to his stablemate Vauban in the Copper Horse Handicap over 1m6f at Royal Ascot. He raced keenly behind a slow gallop and, in the circumstances, did well to finish where he did. That marked him down as an Ebor type and he duly won that contest in August (following one disappointing run over hurdles in between) where, under an inspired Dettori ride, he managed to get the better of the favourite Sweet William, despite having to contend with a wide draw. He ran another cracker in the Melbourne Cup on his next outing in November, finishing seventh of 23 runners, comfortably ahead of Vauban who finished fourteenth.

He next ran over hurdles over Christmas but was pulled up in unsuitable heavy going at Leopardstown, an effort which can easily be forgiven. He then ran okay behind Ballyburn in a Grade 1 at the Dublin Racing Festival on soft to heavy ground in early February and he may take in one of the big festivals over the Jumps in the spring, but after that he will surely be switched to the Flat again and he already looks an ideal type for the Irish St Leger, which is run over 1m6f in September. Another tilt at the Melbourne Cup may also be considered but, whatever targets are chosen for him, this progressive gelding looks sure to rack up further wins. WILLIE MULLINS

## ALIGN THE STARS (IRE)

3 br c Sea The Stars - Kitcara (Shamardal)

Unexposed 3yo handicappers have been the Johnston staple diet down the years and, although only Charlie's name is now on the licence, it's unlikely that anything will change in that respect in the near future. Align The Stars showed form bordering on useful in three starts as a juvenile from 1m to 1m2f and, given the stamina in his pedigree, he could be the type to run up a sequence once he gets to tackle 1m4f and possibly beyond. He's yet to tackle a sound surface (his runs have been on good to soft, soft and Polytrack) but there's no reason why he shouldn't prove as effective on quicker ground and this brother to Group 3 winner/Group 2 placed Al Aasy, who won from 1m2f-1m5f, is capable of leaving the bare facts of his juvenile career behind at some stage. CHARLIE JOHNSTON

## ALMAQAM

3 b c Lope De Vega - Talmada (Cape Cross)

Ed Walker, who has held a training licence for the best part of fifteen years, has trained over 500 British Flat winners in that period and has a deserved reputation for improving his horses. Almaqam is one of the many unexposed 3yos in his care and he is open to progress judged on his encouraging display in a Newmarket novice on his debut in October. Despite showing greenness, this half-brother to Listed-placed 7f-8.6f winner Saleymm picked up well in the last quarter mile to finish fourth of twelve behind previous winner Feigning Madness at odds of 25-1. He should have no problem with 1m2f and, while he'd have to improve to win a similar event at one of the better tracks, this Irish Derby entry should come into his own once he's qualified for a handicap mark. That debut run came on soft ground but his aforementioned half-brother proved smart on a sound surface. ED WALKER

## AL MUSMAK (IRE)

3 b c Night Of Thunder - Parton (Kitten's Joy)

A 95,000gns yearling, Al Musmak got his career off to the perfect start over 7f at Ascot in July where he got the better of the favourite Under The Sun, despite rearing as the stalls opened. The pair drew well clear of the remainder and his rider David Egan said afterwards: "He's got a bit of a knee action and I think a bit of ease in the ground just helped him get on top in the last furlong. I think he's next year's horse and should step forward for the run." He reappeared just two weeks later in a Listed race over the same C&D and he ran well again despite finishing four lengths behind Rosallion, who would frank the form later in the season by winning a Group 1 in France. Behind Al Musmak were Ancient Wisdom, Alnayaabi and Dancing Gemini, who would all go on to win their next outing. Al Musmak also won his next start, this time a Listed race over 1m at Haydock in September, although he probably didn't have to improve much. This time Ben Curtis rode him and he said: "It was very pleasing. He floated across the ground and that was probably the question mark as the ground up until now has been a bit slower, but he handled that beautifully. He has the right mind for it and he took it well." His final assignment was the Group 2 Royal Lodge Stakes at Newmarket, where he finished second behind Ghostwriter, who was completing a hat-trick. The third home was the highly-touted Capulet, so the form stacks up. He was not seen again but he looks a promising type for the year ahead, with Group races at around 8-10f on ground with a bit of cut no doubt on the agenda. ROGER VARIAN

## ALBASHEER (IRE)

*6 ch g Shamardal - Mutebah (Marju)*

Sixth in the 2020 Dewhurst Stakes behind St Mark's Basilica for Owen Burrows, Albasheer's career didn't really progress at three and, after two disappointing runs for that trainer in 2021, he wasn't seen again for about 18 months. Following an underwhelming first run for his new handler Archie Watson in April of last year, he was soon gelded and he gradually began getting his career back on track afterwards. Having been rated 112 at the end of his 2yo season, his mark had fallen to 95 by August of last year and he was able to take advantage by winning a Class 2 Heritage Handicap at York over 6f, albeit in a dead-heat with the veteran Summerghand. Three more good runs in big-field handicaps followed, notably his fourth place in the Ayr Gold Cup in September, in which he finished fast to be beaten less than one length by the winner Significantly. He was switched to the AW afterwards and, following a good third in a 6f Listed race behind Tacarib Bay at Newcastle in November, he ran out a decent winner of a handicap over the same C&D on New Years Day. No doubt all of the big sprint handicaps will be on the agenda for him throughout the summer and, now that he has found his groove again, you wouldn't be too surprised if he were able to win one. ARCHIE WATSON

# ALYANAABI (IRE)

*3 b c Too Darn Hot - Alyamaama (Kitten's Joy)*

If Alyanaabi either catches City Of Troy on an off day or can be kept away from him in the early months of the season, there's a reasonable chance he could pick up one of the colts' 2,000 Guineas judged on the form he showed as a juvenile. He looked a smart prospect when justifying strong market confidence on his debut over 6f at Salisbury last June but, although he was unable to follow up in a Listed event at Ascot when upped to 7f the following month, he shaped better than the bare form in a race that worked out exceptionally well; the winner, Rosallion, going on to win the Group 1 Prix Lagardere on Arc Day, the runner-up Al Musmak taking a Listed event next time and the third, Ancient Wisdom, winning the Autumn Stakes at Newmarket as well as the Group 1 Kameko Futurity at Doncaster in October. Alyanaabi stepped up to the tune of 10lb on Racing Post Ratings when getting up late to win the Group 3 Tattersalls Stakes at Newmarket two months later, staying on powerfully in the closing stages (having met trouble) to get his head in front in the final stride. That effort confirmed him as a potential top-notcher and he was allowed to take his chance against City Of Troy in the Group 1 Dewhurst Stakes only 16 days later, on what would be his first start on a soft surface. Although he was put in his place by the winner, that one is an exceptional sort and the Owen Burrows runner again showed improved form on the figures. He's just the sort to make further progress over the winter and, although connections will undoubtedly be keen to land the first colts' Classic at Newmarket, the percentage call may be to sidestep another match with City Of Troy and he may be worth aiming at the 2,000 Guineas at the Curragh or at Longchamp. Whichever route is taken in the spring, he looks likely to take a hand in several of the leading 3yo contests around 1m and/or 1m2f as the season progresses.

OWEN BURROWS

## AMERICAN BAY

*3 ch c New Bay - All I Need (Peintre Celebre)*

This New Bay colt was far too green to do himself justice over 6f at Newbury on his debut in July but he caught the eye when finishing a nose behind Dragon Leader in a 6f Salisbury novice just three weeks later, with the front pair pulling about four lengths clear of the remainder. It was a particularly noteworthy effort given that he was hampered soon after the start and he again took a ferocious hold in the early stages. The form was franked too with the winner bolting up a 22-runner sales race on his next start and there were also next-time-out wins for the fourth and fifth. American Bay 'only' finished third behind Ghostwriter in a 7f novice stakes at Ascot in early September but the winner, who now has an official rating of 109, would go on to take the Group 2 Royal Lodge Stakes on his next outing, while two horses who finished well behind American Bay would also go to boost the form by winning races next time out. His final assignment of the year was a 7f Kempton novice in October, in which he finished a neck behind Tchaikovsky, with the pair pulling clear of the rest. American Bay again took a keen hold in the early stages which may ultimately have cost him the win. It is surely only a matter of time before he gets that elusive first victory and, once he learns to settle, he will surely be able to prove himself to be much better than his current official rating of 83.
HARRY CHARLTON

## ARABIAN CROWN (FR)

*3 b c Dubawi - Dubai Rose (Dubai Destination)*

A 600,000euros brother to 7f/1m winner Everest Rose, Arabian Crown was well backed to make a winning debut in a 7f Sandown novice in early July, but he took too long to get organised and ultimately had to settle for a close-up third behind Starlore, despite finishing on the front foot. The Raceform race reader said afterwards : "He'll know a lot more next time and could step up significantly." Those words proved spot-on as he remained unbeaten on his next three starts, improving each time. Firstly, he got off the mark in a maiden over the same C&D as on his debut later the same month, after which he was sent to Salisbury to contest a Listed race over 1m, which he also won with the minimum of fuss. William Buick said after that run: "Arabian Crown has really progressed from every run he's had, that being the third of his life. Today was a test and he saw it out well. I like the way he does everything." He was given a break after that win and reappeared in October in the Group 3 Zetland Stakes at Newmarket, again over 1m2f, in which he hosed up by five and a half lengths from the Aidan O'Brien-trained Gasper De Lemos. Charlie Appleby mapped out a plan for his colt after the race: "This horse has won a Listed race and won a Group Three and I will put him away now for the year. One of our two previous Derby winners was a decent two-year-old, winning the Solario Stakes in Masar, and this fellow has a slightly different profile. He has a pedigree that suggests stepping up to the mile and a half as a three-year-old will suit him. He is an exciting horse, there is no doubt about it." He is 12-1 in the ante-post lists for the Derby at the time of writing and that looks a tempting price, given those words. We are likely to see him in one of the recognised Derby trials in the spring, possibly the Dante. CHARLIE APPLEBY

## ARMY ETHOS

*3 b c Shalaa - Dream Dana (Dream Ahead)*
A 120,000gns yearling and a half-brother to speedy 2yo winners Operatic and Dynamic Force, Army Ethos was well found in the betting when making his debut in a six-runner maiden over 6f at Ayr in May and he duly scored in emphatic fashion, with next-time-out winner Jehangeer beaten over 3l into second. It was decided to pitch him into much deeper waters for his next

assignment as he contested the Group 2 Coventry Stakes at Royal Ascot in June but he didn't disappoint as he finished second behind River Tiber, beaten just a neck. Bucanero Fuerte, who would win a Group 2 and a Group 1 on his next two starts, was over a length away in third and, as you would expect from the Coventry, plenty of other winners have emerged from the race. Races like the Prix Morny, the Prix Robert Papin and the July Stakes were all being pencilled in for him at that stage but sadly, he was sidelined shortly afterwards and he will return again this season, with a tilt at the Commonwealth Cup back at Royal Ascot reportedly his early-season target. He's certainly one to keep in mind, assuming all is well again after his layoff. ARCHIE WATSON

## ARREST (IRE)

*4 b c Frankel - Nisriyna (Intikhab)*

When it comes to assessing the prospects of Arrest for the forthcoming season, the Gosdens will no doubt be keen on a prolonged wet spell. The imposing son of Frankel, who has a markedly round action, turned in his worst efforts last year when the ground was quick, notably in the Derby (tenth of fourteen, also didn't seem to handle the track) and in the King Edward VII Stakes at Royal Ascot (fifth of six, although the race could have come a bit too soon) in June. Take those below-par runs out of the equation and his record reads an easy win in the Chester Vase (1m4f, soft) in May on reappearance, a comfortable win in the Geoffrey Freer Stakes (1m5f, good to soft, better than the bare form) in August and a fine second behind Continuous in the St Leger at Doncaster when upped to 1m6f on his final start in September. Frankie Dettori, who rode him in the final Classic said: "The race went exactly like I thought, I was in a good spot, I got him in a good rhythm. Between the three and the two when I passed Gregory I thought 'I could win this' then with my second glance I saw Ryan and I thought 'No, I'm not going to win this!' Arrest was a bit gassy and he'll be a force to be reckoned with next year over a mile and a half - but then it will not be my problem!" Given his physique and his connections, it'll be a surprise should the form he's shown so far prove to be the ceiling of his ability and he's just the type to win at the highest level granted some cut in the ground. Given that older horses have a decent record in the King George VI And Queen Elizabeth Diamond Stakes, he would have leading claims if the ground comes up soft at Ascot in July. JOHN & THADY GOSDEN

## AT VIMEIRO (GER)

*3 bb g Sea The Stars - Amorella (Nathaniel)*

Although he disappointed when favourite at Newmarket on his final start, Jane Chapple-Hyam looks to have a promising sort in the shape of At Vimeiro, who showed enough on his first two starts to suggest that he'll be winning races this year. His debut fifth over a mile (soft) at Doncaster in September was an eyecatching effort, keeping on well in the last quarter mile, having run green, to finish less than four lengths behind God's Window, who went on to finish an excellent third in the Group 1 Kameko Futurity over the same course and distance the following month. That debut form was also franked by the next-time-out wins of the fourth and the sixth. At Vimeiro was raised a fair way in grade on his next start in the Group 2 Royal Lodge Stakes on completely different ground at Newmarket and he showed improved form, despite only finishing seventh. He may not have been over the exertions of that event when disappointing back on soft ground at Newmarket when last seen but he's since been gelded and is well worth another chance. His pedigree suggests that he'll come into his own when he goes up to middle distances. JANE CHAPPLE-HYAM

## AUGUSTE RODIN (IRE)

*4 br c Deep Impact - Rhododendron (Galileo)*

About ten days after winning the Breeders' Cup Turf at Santa Anita, his fifth Group 1 victory in just over a year, Aidan O'Brien and the Coolmore team announced that they would be keeping this son of Deep Impact in training in 2024, which was something of a surprise as he had been widely expected to start a new career as a stallion. Aidan O'Brien said: "Anything from a mile and a quarter to a mile and a half is open to him, he seems to be very comfortable over those sort of trips and it's very exciting to have him back next year. He came back from Santa Anita in great shape and everyone is delighted with him. He'll have a rest now and we'll bring him back early next year. He looks like a horse who could be even more exciting next year so we're all looking forward to it." Given that he won the English and Irish Derbies, the Irish Champion Stakes and the Breeders' Cup Turf in the space of six races in 2023, hearing his trainer say that there may be even more to come should have us all licking our lips in anticipation and one can only hope that this bold move is rewarded with further victories at the top level. AIDAN O'BRIEN

## AULIS

*3 b g Ulysses - Redstart (Cockney Rebel)*

Although Aulis didn't manage to add to his yard's solid 20% strike-rate with juveniles in 2023, Aulis showed enough to suggest that he'll be one to keep an eye on in ordinary handicaps this time round. He wasn't seen on a racecourse until November but he shaped well over 7f on heavy ground after a slow start, making up ground in the last quarter mile to finish sixth behind a promising newcomer in The Reverend (also included in these pages). He stepped up to a mile on Polytrack at Kempton on his next outing and bettered that form when finishing third to a Richard Hughes-

trained improver. The son of Ulysses has since been gelded and, judging by his pedigree, he'll come into his own when upped to 1m2f this year. He's open to improvement and, although he needs one more run to get a mark, he's one to keep a close eye on.
RALPH BECKETT

## AZAZAT (IRE)

*4 b f Camelot - Azama (Sea The Stars)*

This Camelot half-sister to useful stable companion Azallya had a busy time of it at three, running seven times between April and October. Her third place behind the O'Brien pair Savethelastdance and Boogie Woogie over 1m2f at Leopardstown in April looked disappointing at first glance, but the form would be franked with the winner landing the Irish Oaks and the runner-up also taking Listed honours later in the year. Azazat duly won her maiden over 1m4f at the same course the following month and she was next pitched into a Group 3 over the same trip at Cork, where she was narrowly denied by Rosscarberry, with the pair pulling clear of the field. She may have been a shade unfortunate too as her rider was forced to wait for the gaps to open up in the closing stages and she was also slightly hampered near the finish. She next ran in the Irish Oaks and it was a strange race as she looked like she was going best of all as she made her effort early in the straight but she gradually weakened out of it from the 2f pole and perhaps the soft ground caused her not to quite get home. She ran three good races afterwards, finishing second in a pair of Listed races plus a decent fifth of eleven in the Group 3 Dubai Stakes at Newmarket, where she didn't look at home on the track. Currently rated 101, she can win Listed and minor Group races at four, with 1m4f on good to soft ground appearing to suit her ideally.
DERMOT WELD

## BIG EVS (IRE)

*3 b c Blue Point - Hana Lina (Oasis Dream)*

Hands up! If someone had said "Appleby will have a winner at the Breeders' Cup" how many would have thought Mick Appleby, rather than Godolphin's Charlie, was the trainer in question? Probably not many but the Rutland trainer achieved the feat with his first ever runner at the meeting courtesy of speedball Big Evs, who justified favouritism in the Juvenile Turf Sprint over 5f. But back to the beginning. While his debut run at Redcar in late May was encouraging, he didn't really leave the impression that he'd quickly make up into a smart performer, but he turned in a vastly improved effort to win the Listed Windsor Castle Stakes at Royal Ascot on his next start and he followed up in the Molecomb Stakes at Goodwood's Glorious meeting. A step up to Group 1 company against his elders proved a step too far in the Nunthorpe at York in August but he quickly bounced back when landing the Group 2 Flying Childers at the St Leger meeting at Doncaster in September. The sharp 5f turf track at Santa Anita looked sure to suit this ultra-speedy type and that's how it played out in the Breeders' Cup race, where he helped to force strong fractions and, although his lead was dwindling in the closing stages, he had enough left to bag a success at the highest level. He's only raced over 5f so far but he handles most ground and no doubt his main target in the first half of the season will be the Kings' Stand at Royal Ascot. Horses of his age group don't have a great record in that Group 1 in recent times but he's already proven himself at the meeting and he'll be a danger to all if lining up in top form. He's reportedly done well physically over the winter and is one to look forward to this year. MICHAEL APPLEBY

## BLUEDRUM (IRE)

*3 b f Blue Point - Drumfad Bay (Acclamation)*

A homebred Blue Point filly out of a Listed winner, Bluedrum looks like she has a very nice future based

on her one run in a 7f Naas maiden last autumn. She had a good position throughout and she quickened off it to win by two and a half lengths from Keeper's Heart and Chicago Critic, who would both boost the form by winning their maidens next time out. Bluedrum was quite professional too in the way she went about things and she was not at all flattered by the margin of victory. She is likely to be stepped up to 1m at three and she could be exciting.
JESSICA HARRINGTON

## BOLD ACT (IRE)

4 b g New Approach - Dancing Sands (Dubawi)
Further Group race success surely awaits Bold Act in 2024, following his first Group 3 victory at Keeneland (1m4f) in October, which rounded off a good 2023, in which he recorded three wins from seven outings. He started off by winning a 1m conditions event at Chelmsford, where he did well to get his head in front in a race which probably wasn't run to suit. His only below-par run of the season came at Newmarket a few weeks later in the Listed Feilden Stakes but he quickly bounced back with an excellent second behind Bertinelli in a strong renewal of the London Gold Cup at Newbury (1m2f) and he followed that with placed efforts in the Group 3 Hampton Court Stakes over the same trip at Royal Ascot and the Group 2 Prix Eugene Adam at Saint-Cloud, which was won by Horizon Dore, who landed the Prix Dollar two starts later. He regained the winning thread in a Listed race at Deauville in August and he rounded off his year with that win at Keeneland. A real top-of-the-ground horse, Bold Act will no doubt continue his globe-trotting ways and it seems likely that his powerful team will place him to good effect throughout the year.
CHARLIE APPLEBY

## BOTANICAL (IRE)

*4 b g Lope De Vega - Bloomfield (Teofilo)*

The distinctive yellow and black colours of Sheikh Mohammed Obaidh Al Maktoum were seen to good effect on British racecourses last year with just shy of 50 wins, including a memorable top-flight victory at Royal Ascot with Triple Time, who caused a shock when beating super filly Inspiral in the Queen Anne. The owner had 17 horses with a Raceform Rating of 100 or over in 2023, one of them being Botanical, who has the potential to develop into a Group-class performer this season. Although both his wins came with give in the ground at Hamilton, the manner in which he disposed of the 92-rated Mr Professor on his final start in a 0-105 handicap on only his fifth start bodes well for his prospects. Although he's favourite for the Lincoln at the time of writing, his pedigree suggests he'll be at least as good over 1m4f and he ran well on quicker ground at Ascot on his penultimate start in September, when sporting a first-time hood (which was left off for his final start). His trainer is adept at getting the best out of this type of horse and he's one to keep a close eye on. ROGER VARIAN

## BUCANERO FUERTE

*3 b c Wootton Bassett - Frida La Blonde (Elusive City)*

A 165,000euros brother to Wooded and Beat Le Bon, Bucanero Fuerto was weak in the betting when lining up for a 5f Curragh maiden in March of last year but he proved the market all wrong as he won convincingly and, even at that early stage of his career, the Raceform race reader described him as 'Royal Ascot material.' That assessment proved spot-on as his next assignment three months later was the Group 2 Coventry Stakes in which he acquitted himself with great credit as he finished third of twenty behind River Tiber and Army Ethos. Just two weeks later he opened his Group 2 account by taking the

Railway Stakes over 6f back at the Curragh, where he was ridden positively to edge out Unquestionable, who would go on to win the Breeders' Cup Juvenile Turf later in the year. That pair drew well clear from the remainder too. The form was upheld in Group 1 company six weeks later as Bucanero Fuerte beat the Albany Stakes winner Porta Fortuna by 4l in the Phoenix Stakes, again over 6f at the Curragh, with Unquestionable back in fourth. His final assignment of the year came in the National Stakes over 7f where he finished a disappointing third of four behind Henry Longfellow and Islandsinthstream. However, the presence of stablemate Cuban Thunder, who set a brisk gallop, backfired as Bucanero Fuerte became lit up and he was a spent force with well over a furlong to run, suggesting that it was not his true running. It will be interesting to see how he is campaigned in 2024 - Wooded was better at sprint trips while Beat Le Bon won over a mile, so perhaps he will appear in a Guineas trial in the spring and, if that doesn't go to plan, the Commonwealth Cup would no doubt become a viable target. Either way, his trainer Adrian Murray described him as 'a horse of a lifetime' and hopefully he can notch a few more Group races along the way.
ADRIAN MURRAY

## CAPULET (USA)

*3 b c Justify - Wedding Vow (Galileo)*

The decision to mate unbeaten US Triple Crown winner Justify with daughters of super-sire Galileo has reaped instant rewards with a glut of winners, including last year's champion juvenile City Of Troy. Aidan O'Brien's Capulet, who is also bred on that line, has some way to go before matching the level his illustrious stable companion has already achieved but he's a smart sort in his own right and very much the type to win in Pattern company this time round. On the back of a well-supported debut win at Dundalk in mid-August where he made much of the running, he was quickly stepped up in trip and ran with credit in Group 2 turf events at Leopardstown (formerly the Golden Fleece) and at Newmarket (the Royal Lodge). Given the way he saw out both of those races and that he's from the family of Derby winner Serpentine, there's a good chance that the step up to 1m2f and beyond will bring about a fair bit of improvement and he could be one for a Derby Trial before going up to the Derby distance of 1m4f. Whether he's good enough to make his mark at the highest level remains to be seen but he's open to plenty of progress after only three starts and he'll likely make his mark in 2024. AIDAN O'BRIEN

## CARLA'S WAY (IRE)

*3 ch f Starspangledbanner - Sulaalaat (New Approach)*

A £350,000 breeze-up purchase in April of last year, Carla's Way quickly started justifying that hefty price-tag by running out a convincing winner of a 6.5f Doncaster maiden in early June, where she beat subsequent dual winner Star Of Mystery by two and a quarter lengths in a fast time. She was sent off favourite for the Albany Stakes at Royal Ascot just three weeks later but, having carried her head to one side and appearing to hang, she was soon in trouble once the race really took shape, ultimately finishing eighth behind Porta Fortuna. Given wind surgery afterwards, she next appeared in the Group 3 Prestige Stakes at Goodwood in late August where she ran really well to finish second behind Darnation despite the ground, officially described as soft, not being her bag at all. Back on good to firm ground a month later, she hosed up in the Group 2 Rockfel Stakes at Newmarket, where she beat Shuwari and Ylang Ylang by two and a quarter lengths and four and three quarter lengths respectively. That pair would go on to royally boost the form by finishing second and first in the Group 1 Fillies'

Mile at the same course just over two weeks later. Carla's Way was next sent to contest the Breeders' Cup Juvenile Fillies Turf at Santa Anita in early November but that race didn't go her way at all as she finished seventh of the fourteen runners behind Hard To Justify. She was short of room early on before getting caught out wide and she then failed to handle the sharp turns, but despite all that she was only 3l behind the winner as they crossed the line. It's best to forgive her that effort and instead look forward to a productive season as a 3yo - she is around 20-1 for both the English and Irish Guineas at the time of writing, odds which look generous when you consider that Shuwari and Ylang Ylang are both available at about 10-1 Whatever happens there, she looks to have a big future. SIMON CRISFORD

## CAROLUS MAGNUS (IRE)

*6 b g Holy Roman Emperor - Izola (Beat Hollow)*

There's obviously a risk putting a horse up for a list of this nature when the animal in question hasn't won for over two years. However, Carolus Magnus showed more than enough on occasions last year to suggest that he's firmly one to keep onside - notably when a fast-finishing ninth (of 34) to Astro King in the ultra-competitive Cambridgeshire at Newmarket in autumn. Fast ground looks essential to his prospects judged on his overall record and his latest effort when returned to Newmarket in early November can safely be overlooked on account of unsuitably heavy ground. That Cambridgeshire track does seem to suit him though, as both his career wins were gained there in 2021 when he was trained by Andrew Balding. He starts the season on a good mark (6lb lower than at the start of last year), he's probably in his element over 1m2f and it'll be a surprise if he doesn't win a race or two this year for his shrewd trainers when he gets favoured ground conditions. MICHAEL & DAVID EASTERBY

## CATCH THE PADDY (IRE)

*4 b c No Nay Never - Pandora's Box (Galileo)*

Although Catch The Paddy had an in-and-out season in 2023, the manner of his win at Newmarket in late September is still relatively fresh in the mind and, given his physique (he's a scopey sort) he's just the type who could develop into a smart handicapper in the coming months. Kevin Ryan's colt started the season off promisingly enough at York in May but he struggled with consistency until things dropped right for him over 7f at Newmarket. The return to a mile on his AW debut after a short break in November didn't bring about any improvement and he may well concentrate on turf this season. His style of racing means he'll always be suited by having a decent gallop to aim at and, although he seems to stay a mile, he'd be one to bear in mind if connections elected to aim him at a race like the Victoria Cup over 7f at Ascot in May. His only run over 6f last season resulted in his worst effort, but his trainer has done well in the top handicaps over that trip and there's no reason why a strongly run race over that distance - especially at a stiff track like Ascot - shouldn't play to his strengths. Yes, I'm thinking each-way Wokingham chance! KEVIN RYAN

## CHESSPIECE

*4 b c Nathaniel - Royal Solitaire (Shamardal)*

A 100,000euros yearling out of a Group 2-winning mare, Chesspiece won a 1m2f Newcastle maiden in November of 2022 which worked out well and he made a satisfactory return to action in April at Newbury over the same trip, already looking in need of a much stiffer test. He was stepped up to 1m4f at York a month later and resumed winning ways in a handicap, after which he was switched from Rabbah Racing to Godolphin, becoming the first Simon Crisford-trained horse to race in those famous blue silks. He ran a race full of promise on his first start for his new owners in the Group 2 Queen's Vase over 1m6f

at Royal Ascot, where he finished third behind Gregory and Saint George. He then showed a good attitude when winning a 1m4f Listed race at Hamilton in July, after which Crisford nominated the St Leger as the main target with one race in between. That race was the Group 3 Gordon Stakes at Goodwood in which he finished a neck second behind Desert Hero, having tried to make most and Crisford said afterwards: "The St Leger dream is still alive." Sadly, that dream didn't come true as he trailed in sixth of nine runners behind Continuous, finishing 10l behind Desert Hero, who finished third. It clearly wasn't his true form and he bounced back to something like his best at Ascot on his final run of the year, finishing second to the progressive Middle Earth, who had finished just behind him at Doncaster. There are definitely Pattern races to be won with Chesspiece at four with 12-14f on good to soft ground appearing to suit him ideally.
SIMON CRISFORD

## CITY OF TROY (USA)

*3 b c Justify - Together Forever (Galileo)*

Aidan O'Brien is the greatest Flat trainer of this and possibly any generation, with horses like Galileo, Yeats, Rip Van Winkle, Hawk Wing, Giant's Causeway, Rock Of Gibraltar and Stravinsky all names that trip off the tongue. However, after City Of Troy won the Dewhurst Stakes at Newmarket in October to make it three bloodless victories from three outings as a juvenile, O'Brien went on record to say: "There is no doubt he is the best two-year-old I've trained. I've never had a horse that never gets tired. I've never had a horse where we don't know where the limit is. We usually push them to the limit, but we can never find his limit." Based on that quote alone you cannot leave this horse out of a list of potential winners for 2024, although you probably won't get very rich backing him. Ante-post lists for this season's Classics are dominated by this son of Justify - he's evens for both the 2000 Guineas and the Irish Derby at the time of writing, while he's just 6-4 for the Irish 2000 Guineas and 5-2 for the Epsom Derby and it's now just a case of waiting to see which races he runs in, assuming he stays fit and healthy. To put his Dewhurst performance into perspective, his rating of 125 is only 1lb below what Frankel achieved when beating Roderic O'Connor in the same race in 2010. It could be that we have another Frankel on our hands and perhaps City of Troy will be the first horse people mention when they talk about Aidan O'Brien's achievements in years to come. We all love a true equine superstar so let's hope he lives up to that lofty expectation. AIDAN O'BRIEN

## CLANSMAN

*6 b g Nathaniel - Pearl Dance (Nureyev)*

Most horses have a set of requirements that are needed in order for them to show their best form and, for Liam Bailey's Clansman, his prospects seem completely ground dependent. This is highlighted by a quick check at his record which reads 0-17 on AW and ground ranging from good to firm to good to soft, but he's an impressive 4-8 when the ground is soft or heavy. Two of those victories have been on his seasonal reappearance - including last year - so he clearly goes well fresh too. He's fairly versatile trip-wise, having won from 1m2f to 1m7f and, although his latest run over 2m at Newmarket was disappointing (the jockey reported that he "never travelled"), he shapes as though he'll be worth another try over that distance. He's only 2lb higher in the handicap than at the start of last season and he's one to note early in the season when conditions are in his favour. LIAM BAILEY

## CRACKER STAR

*3 b g Cracksman - Pavillon (Showcasing)*

While Richard Hughes has yet to hit the same heights in the training ranks he did as a top-class Flat jockey, he's a shrewd and very capable operator who had his best season prize-money wise in 2023 - thanks in no small part to Northumberland Plate winner Calling The Wind. Hughes has notched a good chunk of over 400 training wins in handicap company and, although Cracker Star may not be a familiar name to most, he's the type who could improve a fair bit once he goes into that type of event. The son of Cracksman never figured in three runs last year but he did compete at Grade 1 tracks such as Sandown and Newmarket (twice) and all three of his runs (over 7f and a mile) threw up winners. He was gelded after his final start, he should stay 1m2f and he appeals as the type to raise his game in 2024.

RICHARD HUGHES

## DANCE SEQUENCE

*3 b f Dubawi - Tearless (Street Cry)*

A Guineas trial in the spring is on the agenda for this Dubawi filly, who was unbeaten in two starts as a juvenile in 2023. She was sent off at a shade of odds-on for her debut over 7f on the July course at Newmarket in the summer and she was just about able to justify that market confidence despite running very green. She was always doing enough though and she was value for more than the winning margin of half a length over the Andrew Balding-trained Upscale. She was given three months off afterwards, making her comeback in the Group 3 Oh So Sharp Stakes on the Rowley course in October, where she got the better of Skellet in the closing stages, having again run green. However, her finishing effort was striking and the form looks strong for the grade. Charlie Appleby said afterwards: "She learned a lot when she won at Newmarket first time and William (Buick) rates her very highly. She's a big, scopey filly and we had this race as a target after that first win so we gave her the time and I think we'll put her away now. It's no secret that we're in a rebuilding process and horses like her are not easy to find. We can dream about running her in a Guineas trial next year." She's around the 20-1 mark for the 1000 Guineas at the time of writing and, with plenty more untapped potential to draw upon, she may be one to keep onside at those sort of odds, especially bearing in mind her trainer's words. CHARLIE APPLEBY

## DANCING GEMINI (IRE)
*3 b c Camelot - Lady Adelaide (Australia)*

Horses like Oxted and Tip Two Win have firmly put Roger Teal on the map in recent seasons and the Lambourn handler looks to have another Group-class colt on his hands for 2024 in the shape of Dancing Gemini. This son of Camelot made a favourable impression when finishing second in a 7f Salisbury maiden in June and he also ran better than his midfield finishing position might suggest in a Listed race at Ascot over the same trip at the end of July. He got off the mark at Newbury on his third start and that maiden looked a strong heat, with subsequent winners Fire Demon and Olympic Candle chasing him home. He then contested the same Listed race at Doncaster that Tip Two Win had won in 2017 before that horse finished runner-up behind Saxon Warrior in the following season's 2,000 Guineas. Dancing Gemini won that Doncaster race convincingly by over 4l from a field of eight previous winners. It was decided to step him up in grade again afterwards but he didn't quite prove ready for it at that stage of his career as he trailed in fifth of seven runners behind Ancient Wisdom in the Group 1 Kameko Futurity Trophy at Doncaster, beaten three and a quarter lengths by the winner. However, he got very tired on the heavy ground, losing two places late on, so he probably ran a little bit better than the bare result implies. He may be aimed at the 2,000 Guineas this spring, but he's middle-distance bred so he could prove better over slightly further in time. He's a 40-1 ante-post shot for the Derby and, granted that the early part of his season goes to plan, he could prove a decent each-way proposition for that race in the summer. Either way, he looks Pattern class and he could become another flag-bearer for his yard. ROGER TEAL

## DEVOTED QUEEN

*3 b f Kingman - Fintry (Shamardal)*

A lengthy, attractive daughter of Kingman, Devoted Queen appeared to know her job well when making a winning debut in a 7f maiden at Newmarket in mid-October. After making smooth headway to get to the front, she showed a good turn of foot to score impressively by two and a half lengths from Vicario. The form hasn't been truly tested yet but So Logical, who was over 5l away in third place, finished a close second in a similar event two weeks later so it probably wasn't the worst race of its type. Devoted Queen has a miler's pedigree - her dam Fintry, who was trained by Andre Fabre, won the Atalanta Stakes at Sandown before finishing third in the Sun Chariot Stakes as a 3yo after winning her only start at two. It's possible to envisage a similar career path for Devoted Queen and no doubt we will see her first in a Guineas trial in April. CHARLIE APPLEBY

## DIEGO VELAZQUEZ (IRE)

*3 b c Frankel - Sweepstake (Acclamation)*

This son of Frankel, who cost a whopping 2,400,000gns as a yearling, was described as 'exciting' after winning a 7f Curragh maiden by nearly 5l in August and, on the back of that he was quickly upped in grade. He proved up to the task as he got the better of stablemate Capulet in the Group 2 Golden Fleece Stakes over 1m at Leopardstown in September, with next-time-out winners finishing third, fourth and sixth. Aidan O'Brien said after that race: "He's still a baby and we were surprised the first day he ran at the Curragh how babyish he was as he never took hold of the bridle. Today he was green as well but a lot better. We think that race will leave him in a very good place." Six weeks later he was sent off second favourite for the Group 1 Kameko Futurity Stakes at Doncaster over 1m but he could only finish sixth of the seven runners, which is, on the face of it, very disappointing. However, there are valid excuses for that below-par run - firstly there had been doubts about the heavy ground at Doncaster beforehand and he never looked at ease on the surface, plus before the race he had to be checked by the vet after his stablemate Battle Cry, who was withdrawn, went down in the stall next to him. Aidan O'Brien said afterwards: "Diego Velazquez got upset. When horses get upset like that in the stalls, their heart rate goes through the roof and usually it goes out the window." It's therefore perhaps best to draw a line through that effort and instead look forward. Presumably his early-season target will be the English or Irish Guineas and after that we can expect him to tread a similar path to Auguste Rodin last year, with one of the Derbies a possibility in the summer. If that trip proves beyond him, he is perhaps an ideal sort for the Irish Champion Stakes at Leopardstown in September over 1m2f. There are certainly good races to be won with him and he's well worth another chance. AIDAN O'BRIEN

## DILIGENT RESDEV

*3 b g Due Diligence - Doobahdeedoo (Animal Kingdom)*

First-time out winners have never been a Mick Easterby speciality down the years so it's worth taking note when one from his yard makes a winning debut. Step forward Diligent Resdev, who turned in a performance bordering on useful when beating Eulace Peacock over 6f on at Newcastle in November, in the process defying a starting price of 33-1. After displaying  greenness both in the paddock (unseated rider) and at the start (reluctant to load), the son of Due Diligence lost ground at the start

and refused to settle but he still came through strongly in the closing stages to beat the more-experienced Andrew Balding market leader by a head, with a neck back to another promising newcomer in Sherman Tank, who also features in these pages. That bare form is nothing out of the ordinary but he deserves plenty of credit and he should prove at least as good over 7f. What the future holds for him isn't clear at this stage but there's every reason to think he'll be able to make a fair bit of improvement as he gains in experience.
MICHAEL & DAVID EASTERBY

## DOHA

*4 b f Sea The Stars - Treve (Motivator)*

There can be few better-bred horses in training than Doha, who is by a Derby/Arc winner out of a dual Arc winner, whose sire was a Derby winner. But, having the best pedigree is not always a guarantee to success in this game and the filly looked fair at best on her first two starts at Kempton and when a disappointing favourite on her turf debut at Leicester in September. However, she may just be the type that needs a bit of time and she turned in an improved effort on her final start at Windsor in mid-October, where she relished the soft ground and pulled clear in the last quarter mile to win a maiden by upwards of nine lengths. That form has been franked by the subsequent wins of the runner-up and fourth and, although she hasn't been out since, she appeals as the sort to do better once she goes up to middle distances, with handicaps now an option before connections try to get some Black Type to her name.
RALPH BECKETT

## DOLCE COURAGE

*4 b g Syouni - Valiant Girl (Lemon Drop Kid)*

Despite running green and hanging badly left on his belated racecourse debut at Southwell in October, Dolce

Courage ran out a good winner of a 7f novice stakes, edging out the odds-on shot Vultar who brought a decent level of form into the contest. That race would work out very well too, with next-time-out wins for four of the first six home. Dolce Courage beat another odds-on favourite, the Andrew Balding-trained Leadman, in a novice over 1m at Newcastle on his second start a few weeks later, a race in which the front pair drew more than 8l clear of the remainder. He looked a lot more streetwise on that occasion and gave the impression that there could be a fair bit more to come. He also looks sure to translate his AW form to turf in due course and there is a decent handicap to be won with him at four.

JOHN & THADY GOSDEN

## DRAGON LEADER (IRE)

*3 ch c El Kabeir - Sweet Dragon Fly (Oasis Dream)*

Having cost just £45,000 as a yearling, Dragon Leader earned prize money in excess of £300,000 in his juvenile season to give his owners, Kennet Valley Thoroughbreds, a decent return on their investment with the promise of plenty more to come at three. After winning a brace of Salisbury novice contents in the summer to kick off his career, he took on 21 rivals in a valuable sales race at York's Ebor meeting in late August and he pulverised them, running out a four-and-a-half length winner from Ziggy's Condor, who had created a favourable impression when winning a Pontefract novice by 3l a month earlier. Dragon Leader tasted defeat for the first and only time a few weeks later when finishing second to Room Service in a 17-runner sales race over 6.5f at Doncaster. That was also the only time he encountered soft ground and, while he certainly didn't run badly, it may not have suited him ideally. Back on a faster surface for his final start in the Redcar 2-Y-O Trophy in October, he justified odds of 4-7 in great style, running out a 3l winner of that Listed contest. It probably wasn't the strongest edition of that race but he won in the manner of a good horse and the likelihood is that he will be stepped up to Group company at three, possibly over 6/7f to start with but there's every chance that he could stay a mile in time. CLIVE COX

## ECONOMICS
*3 ch c Night Of Thunder - La Pomme D'Amour (Peintre Celebre)*

Although William Haggas gets his share of debut winners, his runners tend to come on a fair bit from their first to their second outings. Economics has only had the one run so far but there was more than enough promise to be gleaned from it to think that he'll be of interest when he reappears. A son of Night Of Thunder out of a dam who won up to 1m4f, he was relatively easy in the market but caught the eye on his racecourse debut at Newmarket in November, keeping on well to finish fourth behind debut AW scorer Zoum Zoum, who went on to give the form a boost by taking a Listed event in France on his final start. He should be much wiser for that debut experience and, given his pedigree, it'll be no surprise to see him step up in trip when he next sees the track and he's more than capable of picking up a novice event before he either goes handicapping or goes up in grade. That debut effort came on heavy ground but he should prove fully effective in less testing conditions. He looks a reasonable prospect. WILLIAM HAGGAS

## EL DRAMA (IRE)
*6 ch h Lope De Vega - Victoire Finale (Peintre Celebre)*

This six-year-old has now gone twelve starts without winning - a losing run which stretches back nearly three years - but there's still cause for optimism despite those stark facts. His last win came in May 2021 for previous trainer Roger Varian, a Listed race over 1m2f at Chester which featured Earlswood, Yibir and Foxes Tales among the beaten horses and all of those would prove themselves at Group level subsequently. El Drama's next eight runs were all in Group races, five of them Group 1s, which proved just beyond him, but he often acquitted himself with great credit, notably when finishing a neck behind Alfareeq in last year's Jebel Hatta at Meydan in March. He ran disappointingly for Varian the next three times, once at Meydan and twice on these shores, but he was switched to Karl Burke in July and his two runs for that trainer in August were much more like it. First of all, he finished a close second to Al Aasy in the Group 3 Rose Of Lancaster Stakes at Haydock (10.5f), in which he posted a Raceform Rating in line with his very best for for Varian, and he virtually matched that with another second place behind Spirit Dancer in another Group 3, the Strensall Stakes at York over 8.5f later the same month. He wasn't seen again but those two runs strongly suggest that there is still  some life in the old dog and he should be followed in minor Group or Listed races at around 1m2f on ground that is good or good to soft. The Wolferton Stakes at Royal Ascot in June looks like a suitable early-season target. KARL BURKE

## ELEGANT CALL (IRE)

*3 b f Soldier's Call - Elegant Drama (Dandy Man)*

The feature of Elegant Call's three juvenile starts was the amount of improvement she made between each of those runs. A seemingly unfancied 33-1 chance at Hamilton in September on debut, this second foal of a 6f winner ran as though the race was needed, dropping out in the closing stages to finish sixth of the seven runners. While she didn't figure at the finish at Redcar later in the month, she was beaten half the distance she was at Hamilton and the race threw up winners, with the third and fourth both scoring on their next appearances. She was entitled to be a 50-1 chance for her final race at York judged on those first two starts but, on her first run on a soft surface and her first over 6f, she turned in a much-improved effort to chase home the market leader Pilgrim.

She finished clear of the John & Thady Gosden-trained Gamekeeper, who went on to score on AW next time and both the seventh and the tenth home have since won races. It may be that soft ground is the key to her chances and an opening mark of 74 shouldn't prevent her from being competitive in handicap company. She's one to note in the north. TIM EASTERBY

## EMBESTO

*4 ch c Roaring Lion - Dibajj (Iffraaj)*

An impressive debut winner by 6l at Yarmouth (1m) in early May, Embesto followed up in good style a month later over the same trip at Doncaster, with the length-and-a-half margin of victory probably underestimating the authority of his victory as he raced on the opposite side of the track from the three horses that followed him home, while he also took a keen hold in the early stages. The Raceform race reader suggested that he already looked Group class, although his next assignment was the Listed Sir Henry Cecil Stakes, again over 1m, at Newmarket in mid-July. There he bumped into Nostrum, a Group winner at two, who was having his sights lowered on his first start of the campaign, having missed the 2,000 Guineas following a setback. Embesto still looked a potential Group horse as he comfortably beat the rest of the field and he duly proved it about a month later when dead-heating with Mighty Ulysses in the Group 3 Sovereign Stakes at Salisbury, again over 1m. His final start of the campaign was, on the face of it, a bit disappointing as he could only finish fourth in the Group 2 Prix Daniel Wildenstein at Longchamp, having raced keenly from the front before being unable to pick up on the very soft ground. However, the rating he achieved matched the one he earned for his Sovereign Stakes win and the form of the race was subsequently boosted by Belbek, who finished just in front of him in third, when that horse beat The Revenant in a Group 3 at Saint-Cloud on his next start. Embesto looks ready for a step up to at least 1m2f on the evidence of that run and he still has more to offer in Group races at four. ROGER VARIAN

## ESQUIRE

*3 b g Harry Angel - Ladyship (Oasis Dream)*

Although Esquire didn't make his debut until late September, he's already confirmed himself a smart sort judged on his first two runs with the definite promise of more to come. This good-bodied son of Harry Angel started 9-2 third favourite on his debut at Hamilton and created a good impression, overcoming inexperience to beat a reliable yardstick in Amancio over 6f on good to soft. Given the manner of that win it was perhaps no surprise to see him take a big jump up in grade for his next start - a Listed event at York on soft ground. Despite being worn down in the closing stages by market leader Purosangue, he improved to the tune of over a stone and left the impression that he'd be able to pick up a similar event. He was only seen out once after that when floundering in the heavy conditions at Doncaster on Kameko Futurity day, finishing a long way behind Ballymount Boy. A line can easily be drawn through that below-par effort on account of the ground and this physically imposing sort, who should stay 7f, will be worth another chance granted less testing conditions. DAVID O'MEARA

## EUPHORIC

*3 b c Frankel - Blue Waltz (Pivotal)*

A Tattersalls Book 1 graduate who cost 1,900,000gns in October 2022, Euphoric defied a notable drift in the market to win on debut at Navan over 1m in October. The Frankel colt, whose dam won three times over 1m2f for Luca Cumani and was rated 100 at her peak, learnt on the job and just got there to beat Rocking Tree, who was having his third run, by the narrowest of margins.

The form has taken a few knocks since but it's probably wise not to read too much into that as the experience was clearly badly needed. He is entered in the Irish Derby at the end of June and he will likely return in a trial for that race this spring. The further he goes, the better he will be on the evidence of his only run and he's very much one to keep in mind. AIDAN O'BRIEN

## EXOPLANET (FR)

*4 b g Sea The Stars - Gumriyah (Shamardal)*

The winner of a 7f novice at Newbury at two, Exoplanet wasn't able to add any wins in three runs last season but he displayed significant ability each time and he should be able to pick up the winning thread again in 2024. His first assignment came in a strong Newbury novice over 1m2f where he proved no match for Military Order, but he finished in front of Chesspiece, who would win a Listed race subsequently before finishing a neck behind Desert Order in a Group 3. Exoplanet then ran in the London Gold Cup, again at Newbury over 1m2f, where he lost out by half a length to Bertinelli and Bold Act, but he was unlucky not to win as he jumped over a piece of litter, losing his footing, just as he was making his charge from the rear. Quite a few winners emerged from the race too so the form stacks up. Exoplanet was next seen at Royal Ascot a month later, where he finished second of sixteen runners behind Waipiro in the Group 3 Hampton Court Stakes (1m2f), with Bold Act, ahead of him at Newbury, just behind him in third. Neither of the first two was seen again, but Bold Act would go on to boost the form later in the season by winning a Grade 3 in the United States. Hopefully all is well with Exoplanet after his absence (he's since been gelded) and he can quickly make his mark in minor Group company over middle distances at four, provided that the ground is on the quick side (he was withdrawn from a race in April last year because soft ground was deemed to be unsuitable for him). ROGER VARIAN

## FALLEN ANGEL

*3 gr f Too Darn Hot - Agnes Stewart (Lawman)*

Horses like Quiet Reflection, Laurens and, more recently, Poptronic, have put Karl Burke on the map as a Flat trainer in the last few years and perhaps the former jump jockey can now start dreaming of a first domestic Classic success with Fallen Angel, who won one of the key 2yo trials last season, the Moyglare Stud Stakes over 7f at the Curragh in September. That was a third win in four starts for this daughter of Too Darn Hot, who had also won a maiden at Haydock in May and the Group 3 Sweet Solera Stakes at Newmarket in August, which she won in a canter. In between those two runs she finished half a length behind Shuwari in a Listed race at Sandown (also over 7f) and that filly went on to finish second in both the Rockfel Stakes (behind Carla's Way) and the Fillies' Mile (behind Ylang Ylang) on her next two starts, so the form ties in with the best juvenile fillies' form of 2023. Described as a laid-back and uncomplicated filly, Fallen Angel features prominently in ante-post lists for both the English and Irish 1,000 Guineas. Danny Tudhope, her regular pilot, described her as an ideal type for the 1,000 Guineas after her Moyglare Stud Stakes win, adding: "She was very impressive. She deserves that and she's just getting better and better all the time. She's a beautiful big filly and she's only going to improve." KARL BURKE

## FIRST KISS (IRE)

*3 b f Magna Grecia - Kiss From A Rose (Compton Place)*

There was no mistaking the promise First Kiss showed on her debut when third over 7f at Kempton over 7f in November. Although not in the first three in the betting for this novice event, this half-sister to a 7f-1m winner was immediately up against it having lost ground at the start. She proceeded to run green but made ground in the last quarter mile to finish third to Topanga, who had shown plenty of promise on her debut over the same course and distance the previous month. That effort suggested she'll be even more effective once she goes up to a mile (backed up by her pedigree) and she's entitled to improve a fair bit for that initial experience. At this stage she's more of a handicap project but it's not beyond the realms of possibility, given her connections, that she could develop into a very useful sort before the season is out. JOHN & THADY GOSDEN

## FIRST LOOK (IRE)
*3 ch c Lope De Vega - Bilissie (Dansili)*

Bought by BBA Ireland for 340,000euros at the Arqana sales in August 2022 on behalf of the Ecurie Arna Zingteam, First Look wasn't seen in public for over a year afterwards but he made a good impression when finishing three quarters of a length behind a rival with previous experience over 1m on AW at Chantilly in late October. The horse that beat him, Shamrock Glitter, was sold afterwards for 250,000euros and he then finished an excellent second behind Legend Of Time in a Meydan conditions race in January (front pair clear), which is useful form. First Look also ran again a month later and got off the mark over the same C&D as on his debut, albeit in a race he was entitled to win. He gives the impression that he will be suited by trips of around 1m2f as he matures, he should be fully effective on turf and he's open to plenty of improvement.
ANDRE FABRE

## GALEN
*3 ch c Gleneagles - Apache Storm (Pivotal)*

A flashy chestnut son of Gleneagles, Galen made a striking debut in a quality 7f maiden at the Curragh in early July. Racing towards the rear of midfield in

that thirteen-runner contest, he made his effort about 2f out and ran on well to grab second place near the finish, although he had no chance with the ready winner. However, the horse that beat him was none other than City Of Troy, who is now a warm order for both the English and Irish Guineas and Derbies, while the third home, a length-and-a-quarter behind Galen, was Instant Appeal, who would easily win a maiden on his next start. The winning margin was two and a half lengths and City of Troy would go on to win a Group 2 and a Group 1 even more emphatically than that, so, if you take the form literally, Galen looks like an above-average performer at worst. He wasn't seen again in 2023 but presumably he will win his maiden in the early part of the season before being aimed at the Irish Guineas and Irish Derby, for which he has entries.
JOSEPH O'BRIEN

## GAMEKEEPER (IRE)

*3 b c Blue Point - Gamilati (Bernardini)*

A half-brother to Sovereign Prince, who was a 1m Listed winner for Charlie Appleby a couple of seasons ago, Gamekeeper caught the eye when finishing third of fifteen in a 6f soft-ground York novice in mid-October. Racing in midfield, he took a while to get the hang of things, but he kept on well to finish nearly 3l behind the 83-rated Pilgrim and Elegant Call, who had essentially got first run on him. He wasn't given that a hard race so it wasn't surprising to see him line up for a 6f maiden at Wolverhampton just ten days later. He was strongly backed for that eleven-runner contest and he duly landed the odds by two and a quarter lengths from the William Haggas-trained Monfrid. The fourth and seventh from that race both won next time out while several of the other beaten horses have run well in defeat subsequently, so the form looks okay for the grade. Gamekeeper has no fancy entries but he looks a good prospect for his top connections and he should find his niche in good handicaps at around a mile at three. JOHN & THADY GOSDEN

## GHOSTWRITER (IRE)

*3 b c Invincible Spirit - Moorside (Champs Elysees)*

A 100,000gns foal out of a Listed-placed 1m4f AW winner, Ghostwriter gave the impression that he had learned plenty from his debut run at Newmarket (7f) in August despite winning that ten-runner newcomer race by a ready three-and-a-half lengths. He went to Ascot a month later and was again impressive as he defied a 6lb penalty in a 7f novice stakes, making all. That form was advertised a few times by the beaten horses subsequently and Clive Cox was suitably impressed by his charge: "He's coped with his penalty well today and I loved the way he stretched away there. He's clearly going to get the mile well and he's progressed mentally, and physically he's getting better all the time." The Royal Lodge Stakes over 1m on Newmarket's Rowley course at the end of the month was earmarked as his next target and he duly won that Group 2 contest, beating the 103-rated Al Musmak with relative ease. Cox said: "Ghostwriter is improving with every run and that was a big step to take. His dam won over a mile and a half and it's possible he will get that trip, too. He's always been a nice horse, but had a frame to fill as well. This cements what we thought. What next? We'll discuss it with Jeff Smith (owner) but I'd probably be thinking of next year. We've had a couple of foal entries for the Derby before but this is the first potential live chance who we could be thinking about going that way with." He's currently 20-1 for the Epsom showpiece in June and those look tempting each-way odds given his trainer's musings. CLIVE COX

## GOD'S WINDOW

*3 b c Dubawi - Perfect Clarity (Nathaniel)*

In the space of a month and a half in the autumn, God's Window went from being unraced to a credible Classic prospect. This was down to two runs over a mile at Doncaster, the first a soft-ground maiden in which he created a fine impression to beat several more experienced rivals, including a couple of next-time-out winners. He was then thrown in at the proverbial deep end for his second and final start in the newly sponsored Kameko Futurity, where he was taking on proven Group-race performers in Ancient Wisdom and Diego Velazquez. While he was no match for the first-named, he acquitted himself with a good deal of credit, staying on for third place in the closing stages, two lengths off the Charlie Appleby-trained winner. That effort on heavy ground suggests that he should make up into a good-quality performer in 2024 and he should also be effective on less testing ground (although quick ground would be an unknown). He holds an entry in the Irish 2,000 Guineas but, at this stage, his best chance of Classic success could be over an extended 1m2f in the French Derby, a race John Gosden won in 2020 with Mishriff.
JOHN & THADY GOSDEN

## GOLDEN STRIKE (IRE)

*3 b g Calyx - Hot Legs (Galileo)*

Malton trainer Richard Fahey and owner Sheikh Rashid Dalmook Al Maktoum teamed up to good effect with Perfect Power, who won the Group 1 Morny and Middle Park as a juvenile in 2021 and that colt added the Commonwealth Cup at Royal Ascot to his tally of wins at the highest level as a 3yo in 2022. The pair look to have another nice prospect in the shape of Golden Strike, who showed useful form in two runs in autumn, suggesting that there could be a fair bit more to come. He had to settle for third behind Bondy on his debut at

Pontefract in September, but he fared easily the best of the newcomers in that 6f contest. He stepped up on that form over the same trip at Ayr on his only subsequent start on soft the following month, making all and not hard pressed to fend off a 25-1 newcomer. Although the bare form isn't overly strong, he could do no more than win in the manner he did, his jockey Oisin Orr saying: "there was no real pace but I was able to let him lob away in front and when I asked him he's quickened up and done it nicely. I'd say he'll get further in time but for the minute he seems OK at that trip. He's a big, good-looking horse and I think there's plenty to look forward to with him." He will likely go down the handicap route before dipping his toe into Pattern company and it will be disappointing if he doesn't make up into a smart performer.
RICHARD FAHEY

## GREEK ORDER

*4 b c Kingman - Trojan Queen (Empire Maker)*

Roger Charlton is now off the joint-training licence at Beckhampton, leaving son Harry as the yard's focal point. Charlton senior insists it will be business as usual from a working perspective and it's now up to Harry to try and reach the bar his old man set through his exploits with the likes of Quest For Fame, Sanglamore, Cityscape and Al Kazeem. Three of the aforementioned were Khalid Abdulla-owned and the Juddmonte operation has a potentially high-class prospect in Greek Order, who made up into a smart performer last season. Beaten at short odds on his first three starts in 2022 and on his reappearance last year, the Kingman colt, who is from a fine family, opened his account at Sandown over a mile on his handicap debut in May before following up in good fashion from a 5lb higher mark when upped to 1m2f at Newbury following a near three-month break next time. Although he didn't add to his tally after that, he looked a most unlucky loser from a 10lb higher mark in the Cambridgeshire, persistently denied room at a crucial stage and doing well in the circumstances to get as close to Astro King (who got first run from the best draw) as he did. He matched that effort on his first run in Listed company on his final start in November, despite looking ill at ease on the heavy ground. He left the impression that he'd be suited by quicker ground and a faster pace and he could yet win a top handicap before he heads into Pattern company. With only seven races behind him, there's still room for further improvement and he's an exciting prospect. HARRY CHARLTON

## HAYMAKER

*5 b g Muhaarar - Squash (Pastoral Pursuits)*

A career summary of three wins from 20 starts is a respectable total for an exposed handicapper but Haymaker is still of interest given that he's slipped to a good mark now and he also has excuses for a couple of his defeats in the second half of last season. Although he handles soft ground, his three wins have all been over 6f and 7f on a sound surface when either making the running or racing up with the pace, conditions that he didn't get after his fourth placing in a 6f handicap at Epsom on Derby day. Two of his last four starts were over 5f and, while he ran fairly well at Ascot in September, he found 5f on the AW at Lingfield too much of a test of speed on his latest outing in early November. He was poorly drawn but shaped better than the bare result in the Portland Handicap at Doncaster and, for whatever reason, he just didn't run his race at Salisbury on soft ground on his penultimate start. However, as a result of those below-par efforts he now finds himself 9lb lower in the weights than at the start of last summer and, given that he's gone well fresh in the past, he's one to look out for when conditions are in his favour early in the season. HUGHIE MORRISON

## HENRY LONGFELLOW (IRE)

*3 b c Dubawi - Minding (Galileo)*

City Of Troy is Aidan O'Brien's big talking horse for 2024
but a clear second in the pecking order at Ballydoyle is
this son of Dubawi out of dual Classic winner Minding,
who remained unbeaten in his juvenile season and in
any other year he would now be the warm ante-post
favourite for the Derby. He made his debut in July in a
7f maiden which had previously been won by the likes of
Mac Swiney and Australia and he won it with ease from
the twice-raced Mythology, who would go and boost the
form by winning his maiden a week later. Aidan O'Brien
described him as "an exciting type of horse" and Henry
Longfellow lived up to that billing when winning the
Group 2 Futurity Stakes over the same C&D a month
later, where he beat Islandsinthestream by 2l, although he
was value for far more than that as he wasn't doing a tap
in front. O'Brien said afterwards: "He's a classy horse, he's
able to travel and quickens too. He got a bit lazy when he
went there and Ryan caught hold of him and made him
stretch out, that's what he wanted." The Dewhurst was
pencilled in as the next target at that stage but he actually
reappeared in the Vincent O'Brien National Stakes,
again over 7f at the Curragh, where he beat his old rival
Islandsinthestream, this time by 5l, with Phoenix Stakes
winner Bucanero Fuerte beaten by twelve-and-a-half
lengths in third. However, it was an unsatisfactory race
with the runner-up missing the break and the third horse
getting lit up by a front-running stablemate before failing
to see out the trip on the rain-softened ground, which
had also caused the withdrawal of City Of Troy, who had
been declared to run in the same race. O'Brien said: "This
horse quickens, even though his dam won at up to a mile
and a half. He just took off. We'll see what happens, but
that might be his last run of the season." It proved to
be just that and presumably he will now reappear in a
Guineas, perhaps the Irish one so he doesn't have to take

on City Of Troy, who will no doubt go to Newmarket. He's also second favourite for the English and Irish Derby and there is every chance he will see out that trip, given his breeding. AIDAN O'BRIEN

# IBERIAN (IRE)

*3 b c Lope De Vega - Bella Estrella (High Chaparral)*

A 200,000gns yearling whose dam was a sister to Group 3 winner and Oaks third High Heeled, Iberian was an authoritative winner of a strong 6.5f Newbury novice in mid-June, prompting the Raceform race reader to describe him as a "potential Pattern performer." That assessment was put to the test on his next start at Goodwood in early August as he took part in the Group 2 Vintage Stakes over 7f, in which he finished second, 1l behind Haatem. However, he can have that effort upgraded as he tried to come from last place - around the field - and he was strong at the finish. He made amends in the Group 2 Champagne Stakes at Doncaster the following month, as he ran out a 2l winner from Sunway. The runner-up would go on to win a Group 1 on his next start, as would the third-place finisher Rosallion, so the form looks rock-solid. Iberian was sent off the second favourite behind City Of Troy for the Group 1 Dewhurst Stakes for his final assignment of the season, but that race, run on soft ground at Newmarket in mid-October, did not go to plan at all as he trailed in a 9l sixth behind Aidan O'Brien's stable star. He's clearly better than he showed there with his trainer being adamant that he needs better ground. Perhaps it was a mistake to run him in those conditions, although he had got away with similar ground at Doncaster previously. His trainer has said about him: "He'll get a mile no problem, there's plenty of stamina on the dam's side. And he has a great attitude, he does everything so professionally at home." Watch out for him in a Guineas trial in the spring and, if ground conditions are suitable in early May, perhaps the decision by bookmakers to push him out to 50-1 for the first Classic of the season could turn out to be a mistake. CHARLES HILLS

## ILLINOIS (IRE)

*3 b c Galileo - Danedrop (Danehill)*

A half-brother to the top-class Danedream and a brother to three winners including two at Group 3 level, Illinois looked a bright prospect when running out a 3l winner of 1m1f maiden at the Curragh in early October, especially as he ran green and didn't do much in front once sent to win his race 2f out. That victory put him in the Derby picture with his rider Seamie Heffernan describing him as a "beautiful colt," adding: "He has a lot going for him - pedigree, scope, size, action, wind. He was pretty much a steering job." Two weeks later he was sent to France to contest the Group 1 Criterium De Saint-Cloud over 1m2f where he ran a perfectly respectable race to finish third behind his lesser-fancied stablemate Los Angeles, beaten a length and a quarter. It may have been that the ground was too soft for him and Aidan O'Brien was content enough with the performance, saying: "Ryan (Moore) was very happy with Illinois. He's still a baby and will improve plenty." He remains a top prospect and there are Group races to be won with him at around 1m4f, although it seems likely that very soft or heavy ground will be avoided. AIDAN O'BRIEN

## IMPERIAL SOVEREIGN (IRE)

*3 b c Frankel - Imperial Charm (Dubawi)*

Karl Burke had a fantastic 2023 with his juveniles with 71 winners at a strike-rate of 22% including the likes of Fallen Angel, Darnation and Dawn Charger, who all won Group races. Another of his 2yos who may go on to be a Pattern-level performer in 2024 is Imperial Sovereign, who made a winning debut in a 1m novice stakes at Newcastle in mid-December. A son of Frankel out of a Group 1-placed mare, he was well backed for that Gosforth Park event and he didn't have to be asked for maximum effort by rider Clifford Lee to win readily. His jockey said afterwards: "He's still very green and after the race there were some tyre tracks and he just started ducking around, but he'll have learned plenty today. I'd say he'd stay over the mile for now but he'd probably get further. He's a big horse and has a lot of filling and strengthening to do." Imperial Sovereign is related to Queen Anne winner Triple Time (for these connections) and he looks another exciting prospect for Sheikh Mohammed Obaid Al Maktoum, who also has the likes of El Drama, Royal Rhyme and Cold Case in the care of Burke. KARL BURKE

## INDIAN RUN (IRE)

*3 br c Sioux Nation - Just Wondering (Danehill Dancer)*

Indian Run came unstuck behind the impressive City Of Troy in the Dewhurst in mid-October but he's well worth another chance judged on his earlier-season exploits. This half-brother to a 1m4f winner, whose price rose to 75,000gns as a yearling, showed fair form at Newbury over 6f on his debut in July in a race that has since been franked several times. He was one of the ones to boost the form when beating a subsequent winner at Ascot later that month. However, he reserved his best effort for the Group 3 Acomb Stakes at York in August when he overcame Ballymount Boy, who won a Listed event at Doncaster on his final outing. Even that Group win left Indian Run with a fair bit to find in the Dewhurst but he didn't run his race even so, finishing last of the eight runners behind the Aidan O'Brien-trained winner. Indian Run is just the sort to do well over the winter and his pedigree suggests that he'll be suited by the step up to a mile. There's another decent race in him away from the best 3yos this season.
EVE JOHNSON HOUGHTON

## INISHERIN

*3 b c Shamardal - Ajman Princess (Teofilo)*

If pedigrees are anything to go by, we should be hearing a lot more of Inisherin in the coming months. By top stallion Shamardal out of the same owner's Group 1-winning dam Ajman Princess and from a yard that has had plenty of winning newcomers, the colt was allowed to go off at 50-1 ahead of his debut run at Newmarket's Rowley Mile course in September but he shaped with a considerable amount of promise over the mile trip despite failing to settle and was only beaten by the more experienced Bellum Justum, the pair pulling clear of the remainder. Admittedly both the winner and the runner-up were favoured to an extent by their high draws but that effort stamped him down as one to follow and he is likely to be suited by a step up to 1m2f as he matures. He is open to a good deal of further progress and should have no problems winning a maiden or a novice. Even at this early stage, he appeals strongly as the sort to hold his own in better company. KEVIN RYAN

## ISLANDSINTHESTREAM (IRE)

*3 b c Wootton Bassett - A Mist Opportunity (Foxwedge)*

A pleasing winner of a 7f Curragh maiden at the start of June in which he quickened well despite running green and hanging left, this son of Wootton Bassett was quickly upped in grade and he ran well, despite finishing 2l second to Henry Longfellow in the Group 2 Futurity Stakes, named in honour of his sire and run over the same C&D in August. The winner is clearly smart and he proved that next time as confirmed the form, this time by 5l, in the Group 1 National Stakes in mid-September. However, that was a messy race and Islandsinthestream was on the back foot throughout having missed the break. Seven and a half lengths further back in third was Bucanero Fuerte, who had won the Group 1 Phoenix Stakes on his previous outing. Joseph

O'Brien said afterwards: "That was a great run. The winner is obviously high-class, but I think we have a Group 1 colt. We'll have a look at races like the Prix Jean-Luc Lagardere. Islandsinthestream will have no problem stepping up to a mile." His next assignment wasn't a Group 1 but a valuable sales race at Longchamp over 1m on Arc weekend which he won well despite taking a while to find his stride. Three weeks later he went back to France to contest the Group 1 Criterium De Saint-Cloud over 1m2f, in which he finished a gallant runner-up behind Los Angeles, the margin of victory just a neck. Back in third, over a length behind them, was the highly-rated Illinois and O'Brien was already looking forward: "It's frustrating to be just beaten in a Group 1, but it was a good run. He'll have a holiday now and we'll look at Group 1s for 3yos next year. He's a colt we'll probably campaign internationally, as well as at home." The Ballysax Stakes, a Group 3 over 1m2f at Leopardstown in April, looks like a suitable early-season target and it will be fairly easy to plot a fruitful campaign thereafter in middle-distance Group races. JOSEPH O'BRIEN

## ISRAR

*5 b c Muhaarar - Taghrooda (Sea The Stars)*

Like so many Gosden-trained horses down the years, the 5yo entire Israr has improved with age and, if he raises his game this season, he should be able to compete at the highest level. Having graduated through the handicapping ranks in 2022, the choicely bred son of Muharaar got off the mark on his second attempt in Group company last year when landing the Princess Of Wales's over 1m4f on fast ground at Newmarket's July course in summer. The AW didn't show him in his most favourable light after that but he turned in an effort that matched his Newmarket figure when a close second behind Al Qareem in the Group 3 Cumberland Lodge Stakes at Ascot in October, having looked the likeliest winner when hitting the front in the closing stages. He looked well worth a try over 1m2f but, although he ran respectably on his first venture overseas, he found the progressive Spirit Dancer too strong over that distance in a strong renewal of the upgraded Bahrain International Trophy at Sakhir on his final start of 2023 in November. That was followed by a below-par run in a Group 3 over 1m4f at Doha in February but it's probably best to ignore that effort as it was a muddling event run at a slow gallop which did not suit him. He's well worth another chance and presumably he will be aimed at some of the leading events over 10-12f this summer. It won't take much more of a step up in his best form for him to be competing with the top performers. JOHN & THADY GOSDEN

## JUNKO

*5 b g Intello - Lady Zuzu (Dynaformer)*

Junko came of age in the autumn of last season with Group 1 wins in Germany and in Hong Kong and he looks as though he'll be able to hold his own in the leading top-flight events in France and internationally this season. He had looked the type who could dine at the top table sooner than he did given his excellent second to Anmaat in the 2022 Prix Dollar over 1m1f, but he wasn't at his best in his first three starts last year in the Dubai Turf at Meydan, the Ispahan at Longchamp (much further behind Anmaat than in the Dollar) and behind subsequent Arc runner-up Westover in the Grand Prix de Saint-Cloud. A Group 3 win at Deauville in August and a third place in a Group 2 in October confirmed that he was in good heart without being at his very best but he returned to his peak efforts, winning his last two starts. Both were in Group 1 company but, while he had the run of the race in an uncompetitive event on soft at Munich in November, he dispelled any notions about his ability to handle quick ground when successful in the Hong Kong Vase at Sha Tin's big international meeting. That form has been franked by the subsequent top-flight US success of Warm Hearted, who finished third behind him, and it opens up plenty of new avenues, though as a gelding he won't be eligible for all the Group/Grade 1 events. He handles most ground and it will be fascinating to see how he gets on in 2024. ANDRE FABRE

## KALEIDOSCOPE

*3 b f Kingman - Lightening Pearl (Marju)*

A daughter of Kingman who is related to several good winners, most notably 7f Group 3 scorer Lightening Quick, Kaleidoscope made her belated debut in a 1m Lingfield novice stakes in December and she created a fine impression as she put 3l between herself and experienced stablemate Sea Ice with a further gap of nearly 4l back to the third. She appeared to know her job well and she looks a smart prospect for 2024, with Group races no doubt on the agenda before too long. She has no fancy entries but she's a 33-1 shot for the Oaks at the time of writing and she could be aimed at the Musidora Stakes at York in May to test her credentials for that test. The Gosdens have won the York race for the past two seasons with Emily Upjohn and Soul Sister and Kaleidoscope may be just the type to complete a stable hat-trick. JOHN & THADY GOSDEN

## KARMOLOGY

*3 b f Golden Horn - Kamardal (Shamardal)*

Karmology didn't get the credit she deserved at the time, having won a two-horse race on her debut at Ripon (1m) in early September as her rival - the William Haggas-trained Doom - grabbed the bulk of the headlines for being turned over at odds of 1-25. However, more people took notice when she followed up under a penalty on her AW debut at Newcastle a month later and also when Doom won two of her subsequent three starts, including a Listed event at Fontainebleau in late November.

Karl Burke's filly tasted defeat for the first time on her handicap debut (and her first run on soft ground) at Newmarket in late October but she still bettered the figures she'd gained on her first two starts, and the form was franked by the next-time-out wins for the runner-up and fifth. Judging by her physique, there's almost certainly more improvement to come and she could develop into a very useful handicapper at around a mile, though connections will no doubt be keen to test the water in Listed or minor Group company, probably against the girls, at some point. KARL BURKE

## KIKKULI

*3 b c Kingman - Kind (Danehill)*

A quick glance at Kikkuli's pedigree reveals his instant claim to fame - he's by Kingman and is the final foal of Juddmonte mare Kind - which makes him a half-brother to the outstanding Frankel. The 3yo has some way to go form-wise to get into the same stratosphere as Henry Cecil's brilliant colt, but there was a good deal of promise to be gleaned from his only start as a juvenile. That run didn't come until the final throes of the turf season in November but he shaped well to finish second to previous winner Zoum Zoum on heavy ground at Newmarket, form that was boosted when the winner won a Listed event in France a fortnight later. Although he handled the testing conditions perfectly well, he'll likely prove at least as good on a sounder surface and he should be able to win in maiden or novice company before going up in grade. There's a good deal more to come and he's a really exciting prospect. HARRY CHARLTON

## KING OF STEEL (USA)

*4 gr c Wootton Bassett - Eldacar (Verglas)*

King Of Steel, who appeared in these pages last year as one to follow, surpassed all possible expectations in 2023, finishing a gallant runner-up in the Epsom

Derby on his seasonal reappearance (he had been due to take in the Dante at York in May but was withdrawn having become upset in the stalls), winning at Royal Ascot and notching a first Group 1 success in the Champion Stakes back at Ascot in autumn. Transferred from David Loughnane to Roger Varian after his final start last year, this strapping physical specimen got first run on Auguste Rodin and almost caused a 66-1 shock when showing vastly improved form in the Derby and he showed that was no fluke when beating subsequent Great Voltigeur/St Leger winner Continuous in the King Edward VII Stakes at Royal Ascot, despite looking ill at ease on the quick ground (not surprising for such a big, heavy topped horse). Better was to come and he finished an excellent third to Hukum and Westover in a memorable King George VI and Queen Elizabeth Stakes, his effort just petering out in the closing stages. He was returned to 1m2f after that run and finished a respectable fourth in the Irish Champion Stakes (his owner's retained rider Kevin Stott lost his job two days later) before coming good under an inspired Frankie Dettori in the Champion Stakes. Given that the track and the ground were against him in the Breeders' Cup, he lost little in defeat when fifth, finishing further behind Auguste Rodin than he had in the Derby. In view of his physical stature, it will be a surprise if he can't at least reach the same level as a 4yo, though he may not want the ground to be too quick. He's one of many to look forward to this season. ROGER VARIAN

## LADY FLORA

*3 b f Masar - Lady Brora (Dashing Blade)*

There's the Balding stamp all over the unexposed Lady Flora. Not only is she in the care of Andrew Balding, who also trained the dam, that one's sire is Dashing Blade, who was trained by Andrew's father Ian to win three

Group 1s. And even Lady Flora's colours are synonymous with the yard, the familiar black and yellow silks which will be forever associated with Balding senior's former champion Mill Reef, as well as other top horses including Glint Of Gold, Forest Flower and King Of Clubs (the colours then registered to American philanthropist Paul Mellon). But let's not get carried away. Lady Flora has only had the one run - albeit an encouraging one - over 7f on heavy ground at Newmarket last October when finishing third to market leader Shemozzle. She fared best of those held up that day in a race that has since thrown up a couple of winners. A half-sister to Racing Post Trophy winner Elm Park, she will likely be suited by at least a mile and she should have no problems winning a maiden or a novice event before going up in grade. ANDREW BALDING

## LIBERTY LANE (IRE)

*4 b g Teofilo - Cape Liberty (Cape Cross)*

If Liberty Lane has learnt to settle better over the winter than he has done so far in his races, he could develop into a Group performer this year. Although he's out of a dam who won over 1m6f, his hard-pulling tendencies mean he's not as yet been seen over further than 1m2f. He did very well over a mile in the circumstances, running well (fourth) at Newmarket in July and then showing a good attitude to score at Doncaster in September. He was only seen once after his Doncaster success in the competitive Cambridgeshire, where he again took a good hold and he wasn't at his best under a small penalty for the Doncaster win, dropping out of contention in the last quarter mile. He should stay further than 1m2f and the gelding operation after his last run could prove the key to getting him to settle better. He's not fully exposed after just seven runs and he could pick up a decent handicap before going up into Pattern company. KARL BURKE

## LION'S HOUSE

*3 b g Oasis Dream - Muqantara (First Samurai)*

Although his two wins were in fairly uncompetitive events on the AW, Lion's House has shown more than enough to suggest that he's capable of holding his own in stronger company at three. He looked useful on his debut over 6f at Newcastle in November, losing a bit of ground at the start and meeting trouble before picking up well, despite greenness, once asked to come through and win with a bit in hand, the first two home that day pulling clear of the rest. Roger Varian's gelding had little trouble justifying his position at the head of the market on his second and final start of 2023 at Wolverhampton over the same trip four weeks later. Despite hanging left (presumably still green) he kept on well to beat a reliable yardstick in Influence (has since run well) under his penalty, well on top at the finish. Handicaps and possibly a switch to turf now beckon but he's open to plenty of improvement, there's a good chance he'll stay 7f and he should prove capable of winning more races.
ROGER VARIAN

## LOVE DYNASTY (FR)

*3 b f Dubawi - Geisha Girl (Galileo)*

Clipper Logistics have invested a lot of money into horseflesh over the years and they have been rewarded with some fine types such as Group 1 juvenile scorer Rosdhu Queen and minor Group winners Dramatised, Space Traveller and Soldier's Call. Whether Love Dynasty will go on to win in Pattern company remains to be seen but she created a fine impression on her debut at Newmarket - her only juvenile start - in the autumn, leaving the strong impression that she would be capable of holding her own in stronger company. Despite a slow start on what was very testing ground, the daughter of Dubawi kept on strongly in the last quarter mile to beat the Charlie Appleby-trained market leader Dubai Melody in ready fashion. She should have no problems with a mile (and she should stay 1m2f judged on her pedigree), she should be at least as effective on less-testing ground and her next run is eagerly awaited. Should she make up into a Classic filly in spring, the French Oaks over 1m2f could be her most suitable option. WILLIAM HAGGAS

## LUNAR ECLIPSE (IRE)

*3 gr f Night Of Thunder - Princess De Lune (Shamardal)*

Lunar Eclipse, who won the second division of the fillies novice won by Love Dynasty (above) on heavy ground at Newmarket in early November, similarly looks a promising type and she should be able to hold her own at a higher level in the coming months. David Simcock's runners tend to need a run so it's highly encouraging that the daughter of Night Thunder, who cost 350,000euros as a yearling, was able to win on her debut in the manner she did. Despite missing the break and running green, she picked up well under Hayley Turner in the last half of the 7f contest to beat one who had shaped well on debut at Windsor the previous month. Given that she's by a 2,000 Guineas winner out of a dam whose sire won the French equivalent, there's a good chance her optimum distance could turn out to be a mile. She's open to plenty of improvement and it'll be interesting to see how she handles a sound surface. DAVID SIMCOCK

## MILLIAT (IRE)

*3 b f Kodiac - Silent Confession (Mr Greeley)*

A big drifter before the off, Milliat defied that market weakness by winning a 7f Dundalk fillies' maiden in uncomplicated fashion at the end of September, edging out the 86-rated favourite Grand Job. She had easily won a Barrier trial a month earlier so it was rather surprising that she returned an SP of 25-1 having opened up at 10-1. Assistant trainer Brian Slattery said afterwards: "We think she's high class and we're not sure what will happen next. She will probably be for sale but, if not, she will probably go for a Guineas trial. It's all about next year with her. We like her and she's a very good filly. She wants a mile all day. Andrew would love to keep her, we think she's very smart." She cost 30,000euro as a yearling  and she's not been sold yet so look out for her in a Guineas trial in the early part of the turf season - afterwards she should be able to make her mark at Listed or Group level at least. ANDREW SLATTERY

## NIGHT RAIDER (IRE)

*3 br c Dark Angel - Dorraar (Shamardal)*

We've talked elsewhere on these pages about Karl Burke's excellent 2023 with his juveniles and Night Raider is yet another one of his charges to note for 2024 after winning a 7f novice stakes at Southwell by an easy 9l in December. A 155,000gns foal, he's a half-brother to the smart sprinter Far Above and he clearly knew his job at the Nottinghamshire venue, leading over 1f out before scooting clear in the closing stages. The Raceform rating of 95 that he recorded was the joint eighth best achieved by any juvenile in 2023 so it will be fascinating to see what he can do as he is switched to turf in the spring. Burke said the following afterwards: "It was a very impressive debut, he's a beautiful horse and a horse we've always thought an awful lot of. He got a slight niggle early in the summer which meant we had to back off him, but he's very much going to improve from two to three as he's a big horse. He's been working nicely, but he's not one we've really drilled at home, there's plenty of improvement in him. Visually it was a stunning performance and the time and ratings back that up as well, but there's still plenty in the tank for him to improve from two to three." KARL BURKE

## NOTHING TO SEA (GER)

*4 b g Sea The Moon - Nada (Authorized)*

An eyecatching second over 7f in his only run as a 2yo, this gelding still looked a bit raw when he was turned over at short odds in his return over 1m2f at Windsor in early May but he put that run behind him quickly by winning a fourteen-runner Newbury maiden over the same trip just eleven days later. That looked a strong heat too with plenty of winners emerging from it, including Nothing To Sea himself. His victory came over 1m6f at Sandown towards the end of July, a five-runner handicap which he won with authority from the Sir Mark Prescott-trained Brave Knight with the rest of the field well beaten off. His rating went from 91 to 97 after that run but we didn't see him again afterwards. At the time he was described by his trainer as "a little bit heavy" which suggests that he can find further progress as he resumes his career at four. It appears that soft ground is important to him so do not expect him to run when the ground is rattling fast in mid-summer. He's one for decent handicaps and minor Group races at around 2m and he's the type his trainer tends to do well with. RALPH BECKETT

## ONE LOOK (IRE)

*3 b f Gleneagles - Holy Salt (Holy Roman Emperor)*

One of the most visually stunning performances from last year was One Look's debut win over 7f on soft ground in a sales race at the Curragh in September. Although Paddy Twomey's filly was one of only two newcomers in the field, her home reputation meant she started at 5-1 second favourite in the market behind even-money chance Cherry Blossom. However, she absolutely pulverised a decent-looking field, travelling strongly and pulling clear in the closing stages to beat Aidan O'Brien's runner by six lengths. Twomey said: "One Look is a nice filly. I thought I would get her out earlier in the year, but it was just the way things worked out. She was just ready to run this week. I thought she was good enough to be competitive. The plan was to track Frankie (Dettori) on Cherry Blossom and see how we got on. I gave her a Guineas entry this week. It was a big performance to do that and I think that will be it for the year." That form has some substance to it as Cherry Blossom went on to finish fourth in the Cheveley Park Stakes and the third-placed My Mate Alfie ran to a similar level in another sales race on her final start. Judging on the manner of that performance, she looks a potential Classic filly and she's quoted at 14-1 for the 1,000 Guineas and 5-1 for the Irish equivalent. Whether she needs soft ground to show her best remains to be seen but she should stay a mile and she's a most exciting prospect who should be able to hold her own in Pattern company. PADDY TWOMEY

## ORAZIO (IRE)

*5 gr g Caravaggio - Lady Fashion (Oasis Dream)*

A season that began with so much promise petered out in fairly disappointing fashion for Orazio. The Charles Hills-trained sprinter missed the whole of 2022 due to a setback so he was entitled to need his first run for 500 days at Kempton in January. He was off again until the spring but proved a different proposition returned to turf, turning in an effort bordering on smart to beat subsequent winner Probe by a length at Newmarket (6f, good to soft) in April. He looked as though he was quickly making up for lost time when following up on soft ground over the same trip at Ascot the following month, in the process teeing himself up nicely for a tilt at the Wokingham. While he ran respectably in that, finishing sixth of 29 from a 9lb higher mark, he didn't quite look as effective on the prevailing good to firm ground. His next stop was the Stewards' Cup at Goodwood but, while he seems to go well on soft ground, he (like many) was bogged down in ground that turned heavy and he failed to run his race, dropping away in the last furlong and a half. He was a single-figure price for the Ayr Gold Cup on ground (good to soft) that should have been more to his liking but he never got into contention and finished in midfield, albeit only beaten three lengths. His trainer then drew stumps for the season and Orazio has now been gelded. That could prove the making of him and it'll be no surprise to see him get back on track in 2024. CHARLES HILLS

## ORTELIUS (USA)

*3 b c Justify - Milam (Street Sense)*

Although his pedigree is all about dirt, Ortelius has shown useful form in two runs on turf and he appeals as the sort to win races when he gets a sufficient test of his stamina this year. He created a good impression on his debut, just losing out by a head to the Ger Lyons-trained Tamrat over a mile at the Curragh on good ground in August, a performance that suggested he was a shoo-in to win a similar event before the season was out. However, he only saw the racecourse once more, just under one month later, on fast ground at Newmarket. Although he failed to build on his debut form, he again showed a useful level of ability, getting outpaced but sticking on in the closing stages to get within four lengths of Bellum Justum in a race that should throw up plenty of winners. The run can also be upgraded as he was drawn in stall 1, compared to stall 16 for the winner, 17 for the runner-up, 18 for the fourth and 19 for the fifth. He will be suited by at least 1m2f and, although his Irish 2,000 Guineas/ Derby entries are optimistic at this stage, he could turn out to be smart. AIDAN O'BRIEN

## OXFORD COMMA (IRE)

*3 ch f Nathaniel - Abilene (Samum)*

Ralph Beckett had his best season numerically in 2023, with 133 domestic winners yielding prizemoney of over £4m, a figure that doesn't include Westover's huge overseas dividends (second in the Sheema Classic, won a Group 1 at Saint-Cloud and finished second in the Arc). Although Oxford Comma contributed just over £1,000 to the domestic total, it will be a bit of a surprise if her prizemoney tally in 2024 isn't considerably higher. She shaped with a good deal of encouragement when third to Love Dynasty over 7f on heavy ground at Newmarket on her debut in November and she's open to plenty of improvement. Her effort can be marked up a touch too as she fared best of those drawn low and her pedigree strongly suggests that she will come into her own when stepped up to middle distances. Her half-brother (by Lope De Vega) Juan De Montalban proved smart from 1m2f-1m4f and he won on ground ranging from heavy to good to firm, so it's very likely that she'll handle quicker ground given that she's by Nathaniel. RALPH BECKETT

## PER CONTRA (IRE)

*3 b c Footstepsinthesand - Nonetheless (Fastnet Rock)*

Ollie Sangster is an up-and-coming trainer who learned his trade under the tutelage of the likes of Wesley Ward in the USA, Joseph O'Brien in Ireland, David Hayes in Australia and Hugo Palmer & Charlie Hills in Britain. He now has a training base at the historic Manton House in Wiltshire and he has some excellent prospects to go to war with as he embarks on his second season as a trainer in 2024. Per Contra is one such animal - he created a favourable impression when winning a 7f Chepstow maiden in July, having been well supported beforehand. He wasn't entirely straightforward, running green and then drifting badly in the closing stages but it was nevertheless a taking performance to put over three lengths between himself and the runner-up

Loaded Quiver. Plenty of winners came out of that race too, including Per Contra himself who followed up under a penalty over the same trip at Ffos Las a month later,

albeit in a four-runner race he had every right to win. Given some time off afterwards, he was upped in grade for his final start in October as he took part in the Group 3 Autumn Stakes over 1m at Newmarket in October. It was a race which didn't go to plan, however - he was being cajoled along from the outset and then hung badly left once getting into contention before fading out of it to finish a well-beaten fifth of seven runners behind Ancient Wisdom. It's still early days, however, and there's clearly a powerful engine under the bonnet so he can make amends in slightly calmer waters as he resumes his career. He looks just the sort to win a decent handicap at around 1m once he irons out his quirks and a mark of 88 is one that can be exploited by his talented young handler.
OLLIE SANGSTER

## POINT SUR (IRE)

*3 b c Too Darn Hot - Bright Beacon (Manduro)*

While Point Sur wouldn't be at the top of the pecking order for the 3yos at Charlie Appleby's Moulton Paddocks in Newmarket, he showed himself to be a useful juvenile in just two starts in 2023 with the promise of a good deal more to come this season. A half-brother to the yard's New London, who finished second in the 2022 St Leger, he shaped well on his debut over 7f on fast ground at Newmarket in October, a race that threw up several winners. He was one of the subsequent winners when he returned to that venue, but on much softer ground later in the month, showing a good attitude in the closing stages to nail Native Warrior, the pair pulling clear of the rest. He will be suited by a step up to middle distances this season and, if he's to figure in a Classic, it may well be the St Leger given the stamina on his dam's side. Whatever targets are set for him, he's open to a stack of improvement and is just the type to win more races.
CHARLIE APPLEBY

## PORTERS PLACE (IRE)
*3 gr f Make Believe - Shreyas (Dalakhani)*

Although Porters Place didn't register the same lofty figure that stable companion One Look did when bolting up on her debut, she nevertheless marked herself down as one to follow when winning by four lengths over 7f on heavy ground on her debut at the Curragh in October. She was well found in the market - she started the 15-8 favourite - and justified that confidence, pulling clear in the last half furlong to win going away in the manner of a smart filly. Paddy Twomey, her trainer, said: " Porters Place is a nice filly. She's been there all year and we hadn't asked her any questions. Physically and mentally she came to herself in the last month or so and this is a race I like, we won it two years ago and you're not meeting horses who have run lots of times. She was a little bit green but she found her feet and I was delighted with how she put it to bed. I knew she'd be green as we've only worked her twice. Once she got a bit of light, she took off. If we are lucky, we might have an Oaks filly on our hands and we will treat her accordingly." The trainer might have a job keeping his two fillies apart but it's an enviable problem to have and she's the type to take her form to the next level in 2024. PADDY TWOMEY

## PRIMEVAL
*4 b f Lope De Vega - Passage Of Time (Dansili)*

A half-sister to five winners including the smart Time Test and Tempus, Primeval looked to have inherited plenty of ability on the evidence of her debut run in a 6f novice at Doncaster in mid-July as she proved far too strong for the penalised runner-up Couplet inside the final furlong. The Raceform race reader suggested that she could make up into a Listed/Group 3 performer on the back of that but she was kept to novice company a month later at Windsor, again over

6f, as she ran out a narrow winner from the 76-rated Laoisman. She was upped to 7f for her handicap debut at Kempton in September and she was well supported for that contest but it appeared that she didn't quite see out the trip as she faded into fourth behind the subsequent dual winner Cloud Cover. She was tried again over 6f for her next assignment at Newcastle and she looked to be coming with a winning run up the centre about 1f out, travelling best of all, before being swamped by the nearside runners in the closing stages to finish fourth, beaten just over 1l. Perhaps if she had come up the favoured near rail like the three horses that beat her she would have won so it looks an effort that can be upgraded. Solray, who finished just behind her in fifth, would frank the form by easily winning a C&D handicap on her next start and that filly is now rated 85. Primeval is bred to get 1m+ but she is built like a sprinter and perhaps she will be kept to around 6f in the early part of the season. She certainly looks capable of winning off her current rating of 80.
HARRY CHARLTON

## PUTURHANDSTOGETHER (IRE)

*3 b g Caravaggio - Round Of Applause (Galileo)*

Puturhandstogether is now handicapped on the form of three runs over 6f to 1m on turf and the AW but a quick glance at his pedigree suggests he will soon leave what he's achieved so far behind once he goes up in distance. That's because there's plenty of stamina on the dam's side; he's a half-brother to a 2m5f hurdle winner out of an unraced sister to 1m4f-1m6f scorer I Have A Dream. Ironically, his best effort in terms of ratings came on his most recent start in January when dropped to 6f at Dundalk, where he kept on steadily in the closing stages to finish sixth behind Perfect Judgement, form that has already been franked by a subsequent win by the third. That eyecatching run wasn't lost on the handicapper, who allotted him an opening mark of 74 but, given he's open to plenty of improvement, he should be able to win from that sort of rating. JOSEPH O'BRIEN

## REAL DREAM (IRE)

*5 b g Lope De Vega - Laganore (Fastnet Rock)*

Sir Michael Stoute's ability to improve older horses is well documented and it will be a surprise if his 5yo Real Dream has reached the ceiling of his ability after only eight runs. Although he didn't get to the track as a juvenile, he quickly made up into a useful 3yo, running well twice on the AW before winning his maiden at Doncaster in June 2022. He was off for another eleven months afterwards but he looked better than ever on his reappearance last season when winning at Kempton over 1m4f in early May. He then took the step up to 1m6f in his stride when scoring at Ascot in July and, although he ran poorly from a wide draw in the Ebor, he proved his effectiveness on soft ground when a fine third (a career-best effort) in the Mallard Handicap at Doncaster's St Leger meeting in September. He wasn't seen again but he's capable of winning a handicap from his current mark of 99 and he may well be up to scoring in Listed or minor Group company further down the line. He handles a wide array of ground and he seems sure to win more races. SIR MICHAEL STOUTE

## ROOM SERVICE (IRE)

*3 b c Kodi Bear - Tamara Love*

Room Service appeals as a 3yo who should be capable of making his mark in minor Pattern company this year, judged on his emphatic win in the sales race at Doncaster's St Leger meeting in September. Kevin Ryan's colt, who won on his debut at Wetherby in May, ran a fine third in a competitive nursery at York's August meeting (a race which threw up six next-time-out winners) but even that effort didn't suggest that he'd win the Doncaster race in the manner he did. Having his first run on soft ground, the colt travelled strongly before pulling away in the closing stages to break the unbeaten record of market leader Dragon Leader, who franked the form by winning the Two-Year-Old Trophy at Redcar next time. That effort showed Room Service is already a smart sort and his physique suggests he has plenty of scope for further improvement. Whether the improved form is solely down to the soft ground remains to be seen but he should stay a mile and he's an exciting prospect. KEVIN RYAN

## SAMUEL COLT (IRE)

*3 b c No Nay Never - Lesson In Life (Duke Of Marmalade)*

Aidan O'Brien has his usual embarrassment of riches of 3yo colts to aim at the Classics in 2024 and one who arrived on the scene late in the season was this 340,000euros son of No Nay Never, who won a backend 6f maiden at the Curragh by four and a half lengths. He appeared to relish the heavy ground as he pulled readily clear from his nineteen rivals on that late October day but assistant trainer Chris Armstrong said afterwards: "He wasn't in love with the ground but his class got him through it. He could be an exciting colt for next year all being well." The time was decent and back in fourth place, seven lengths behind the winner, was the 84-rated Kortez Bay so Samuel Colt could be very smart if you take that at face value. His breeding suggests that a mile will be his ideal trip so presumably we will see him in a Guineas trial initially before a plan is mapped out for him. AIDAN O'BRIEN

## SEA JOURNEY (IRE)

*3 b f Sea The Stars - Journey (Dubawi)*

Owner George Strawbridge has been a regular feature in the John Gosden yard down the years and there's been plenty of success for him since Gosden's son Thady was added to the licence. The owner's good horses in the last couple of years include Free Wind, Epictetus, Mimikyu and Torito and his Sea Journey looks one who also has the potential to develop into a smart sort over middle distances. Out of Strawbridge's 1m4f Group 1-winning mare Journey (trained by Gosden senior), the daughter of Sea The Stars started as third favourite and showed definite promise on her only juvenile start over 7f on heavy ground at Newmarket in November, despite her apparent greenness. She should be a different proposition with that run under her belt and another winter behind her to help with the maturing process. Despite the stamina in her pedigree, less testing ground will probably be more to her liking (her dam seemed best on a sound surface) and it will be fascinating to see how she develops in 2024. JOHN & THADY GOSDEN

## SHERMAN TANK (FR)

*3 b g Sioux Nation - Pretty Darling (Le Havre)*

Newmarket trainer David Simcock is adept at buying a nice type of individual, i.e. a good-bodied sort with bags of scope for further improvement. One such horse is Sherman Tank, who caught the eye on his debut over 6f at Newcastle on November Handicap day, finishing with some purpose in the closing stages to snatch third place behind Diligent Resdev, who also figures in these pages. A close relation to a 7f AW winner, he can be expected to improve a fair bit for that initial experience. Judging by his pedigree, he'll have no problems with at least a mile and he should prove at least as effective on turf. He's open to a good deal of improvement (he's been gelded since that one run) and he can make his mark in ordinary maiden or novice company before going into handicaps. DAVID SIMCOCK

## SEE THE FIRE

*3 ch f Sea The Stars - Arabian Queen (Dubawi)*

By Sea The Stars out of Group 1 winner Arabian Queen, See The Fire came home best of all to justify good market support on her debut in a 7f fillies' maiden in August, with next-time-out winner Heartfullofstars beaten a length and a half into second. She edged left under pressure, probably due to the strong crosswind, but she appreciated the uphill finish, suggesting that a step up in trip might suit her. She was tried over 1m in the Group 2 May Hill Stakes at Doncaster the following month and she ran another excellent race, finishing three lengths behind the Karl Burke-trained Darnation, who was having her fourth start. She would have finished a lot closer too had she not shied away from the whip when on the heels of the winner inside the final furlong before getting hampered. She wouldn't have won, but for a filly having just her second start that was quite significant interference on soft ground, albeit caused by her own doing, and she was still about four lengths clear of the third. A month later she ran another huge race, finishing third behind Ylang Ylang and Shuwari in the Group 1 Fillies' Mile, beaten just a length and a quarter by the winner. As on her first two starts, she went left under pressure and, with the stalls being on the far side, that was of zero help to her. She still ran well and she has already come a long way in a short period of time. She's from a top family and she's one to look forward to this year - she's one to bear in mind for a race like the Juddmonte International over 1m2f at York in May which her dam famously won in 2015, beating the hitherto unbeaten Golden Horn. ANDREW BALDING

## SHUWARI (IRE)

*3 ch f New Bay - Lady Pimpernel (Sir Percy)*

We've already touched upon the talents of new trainer Ollie Sangster elsewhere in these pages and the horse who could really put him on the map in 2024 is this daughter of New Bay who has an official rating of 110 after four excellent runs in her juvenile season. She made a taking debut in a 7f novice stakes at Newbury in June, travelling well in rear before picking up nicely to overcome Lady Of Leisure, who set a reasonable form standard coming into the contest. A month later she won a Listed race at Sandown over the same trip, beating none other than Fallen Angel, who would win a Group 2 and a Group 1 on her next two starts. She was upped to Group 2 level for her next assignment as she contested the Rockfel Stakes, again over 7f, at Newmarket in late September, where she ran well once more even though she had to give best to Carla's Way. However, the two-and-a-quarter length margin of victory possibly flattered the winner a touch as she raced in the ideal position just off the lead while Shuwari had to come from the rear and she could never make serious inroads on the winner in the closing stages. She still finished nicely clear of Ylang Ylang in third and she took on that rival again in the Fillies' Mile at the same course two weeks later - this time she lost out by half a length on the rain-softened ground. However, she was distracted by the antics of the eventual third, See The Fire, who hung across her, and, having grabbed the lead inside the final furlong, she was outstayed by the Irish-trained filly, who appeared to handle the conditions slightly better. It still represented a career best and her trainer was philosophical afterwards: "Everything went well apart from the fact we didn't win. That will be her for the season and I suppose we will work back from the 1,000 Guineas. I wouldn't be afraid of pitching straight up into a 1,000 Guineas as she is a straightforward filly to train." OLLIE SANGSTER

## SILVER SWORD

*4 gr g Charm Spirit - Aurora Gray (Rip Van Winkle)*

This progressive grey had a busy 2023 with seven runs between April and October producing three wins and two

second places. He opened his account in good style in a 1m Southwell maiden in April, after which he was awarded an opening mark of 82. He ran well off that rating on his handicap debut over 1m2f at Epsom in June, finishing second of thirteen runners behind another progressive sort, Torito - that horse finished a good fourth in the Group 3 Hampton Court Stakes on his next outing and he also makes it into this list. Silver Sword was dropped back to 1m at the end of the same month and, despite taking a keen hold, he won that Pontefract handicap with ease, taking the drop back in trip in his stride. By now his rating had gone up to 93 and he ran okay off that mark at Goodwood in early August, finishing seventh of fifteen runners in a Class 2 handicap over 1m2f on soft ground, which wouldn't have suited him at all. Back on a faster surface at York three weeks later he won the Sky Bet Mile in good style despite, once again, taking a keen hold. That took his rating to 97 and it was decided to pitch him into Listed company in September - he ran a perfectly sound race on unsuitably soft ground to finish fifth behind the 115-rated Chindit, beaten just three-and-a-half lengths. He built on that by finishing second of nine behind Highland Avenue in the Group 3 Darley Stakes over 1m1f at Newmarket in October, which was again run on soft ground. A length and a half behind him in fifth was Spirit Dancer, who would boost the form by winning a Group 2 on his next start. Silver Sword is now rated 103 which means he will probably need to ply his trade in Listed and Group races but there still appears to be improvement in him and there are more races to be won over 8-10f on ground which doesn't have soft or heavy in the description.
DYLAN CUNHA

## SKELLET (IRE)

*3 b f Kingman - Dane Street (Street Cry)*

A half-sister to Group 1 winner Skitter Scatter, Skellet was unable to justify favouritism in a 7f newcomers' maiden at

Sandown in August but she might well have done so had she not been forced to wait for room over 2f out before again being caught in a pocket inside the final furlong. She confirmed the promise of that initial run just eighteen days later at Salisbury by running out a ready winner of a 7f maiden, with next-time-out scorer Serene Seraph chasing her home. Ralph Beckett said at the time:"She's big, tall and gangly. She's a nice filly and one for next year, we could go for the Rockfel but we'll probably take a more conservative view." That Group 2 at the end of September did indeed come too soon for Skellet but we did see her again in mid October in the Group 3 Oh So Sharp Stakes, again over 7f. She ran another cracker in that race, finishing second to Dance Sequence, beaten just a neck, having blown the start and then forging into the lead over a furlong out before being run out of it in the closing stages. She gave the impression that she would improve at three and she will no doubt be running in more Group races at around a mile - the Princess Elizabeth Stakes, a Group 3 over 8.5f at Epson in June, which Beckett won in 2023 with Prosperous Voyage, looks like an ideal early-season target for her. RALPH BECKETT

## SON OF MAN (IRE)

*3 b g Dark Angel - Crisolles (Le Havre)*

Irrespective of whether Son Of Man's long term future is in Britain or in Hong Kong (his owners are a presence in that region), he made up into a very useful sort during his 2yo campaign last year and there's the promise of more to come. A winner on his debut over 6f (good to soft) at Yarmouth in September, connections wasted no time pitching him into Group company and he ran well on both starts in a pair of 7f Group 3s at Newmarket (on good to firm and on heavy), his best effort coming when third in the Horris Hill in November. His season wasn't finished there as he went to France less than a fortnight later, finishing fifth (a bit below his best) behind Ralph

Beckett's unbeaten Zoum Zoum in a heavy ground Listed event. There's a bit of stamina on the dam's side so it's not unreasonable to think Jane Chapple-Hyam's gelding should stay 1m2f this time round. A mark of 95 shouldn't be insurmountable should he be tried in decent handicap company and he won't have to improve too much to make an impact in Listed or minor Group events.
JANE CHAPPLE-HYAM

## SPOKEN TRUTH (IRE)

*3 b c Frankel - Joailliere (Dubawi)*

As a brother to the 2022 Irish 1,000 Guineas winner Homeless Songs, Spoken Truth is indeed a valuable commodity and, although he didn't achieve the level of form that one did as a juvenile, he still shaped with a good deal of promise on his sole start at Leopardstown over 7f in October. He started as 5-2 second favourite in a field of ten and kept on well in the closing stages, despite showing signs of greenness, to finish fourth, one place behind Aidan O'Brien's 89-rated Master Of The Hunt. Given his pedigree, he should have no problems with a mile and, although Homeless Songs wasn't asked to go any further than that trip, as he's by Frankel out of a Dubawi mare, there should be no problems with him staying 1m2f. He's in very good hands and is capable of leaving the bare facts behind at some point. DERMOT WELD

## SURELY NOT (IRE)

*4 b g National Defense - Thanks (Kheleyf)*

Twice a winner as a juvenile in 2022 and gelded at the end of that year, Surely Not made the perfect start to his 3yo career last April by winning a Newmarket handicap over 1m with something to spare and plenty of winners would emerge from that Class 4 contest. He built on that victory by following up at Chester over 7.5f a few weeks later and, once again, the form would be advertised with the third and fourth home both winning their next outing. A new mark of 92 meant that he was able to run in the Britannia Handicap over 1m at Royal Ascot and he ran another blinder in that, finishing sixth of the 29 runners despite being denied room at a crucial stage and being forced to switch to his left. He was a clear second best on his side of the track (behind the winner of the race, Docklands) and he certainly looked to have progressed again. Sadly that was the last we saw of him in 2023 but, assuming all is well with him, he can pick up where he left off this spring. His rating has been left unchanged at 92 and there is a decent handicap to be won with him at around 1m, with all ground appearing to come alike to him. DOMINIC FFRENCH DAVIS

## TAYMURA (IRE)

*4 b f Siyouni - Timabiyra (Linamix)*

Taymura has only shown a modest level of ability in two starts but she appeals as the sort to do better in handicaps in 2024. Dermot Weld's filly started off over 1m1f at Leopardstown in October and ran respectably, keeping on in a manner that suggested that she'd be suited by further. Her trainer wasted no time in stepping her up in trip and she ran to a similar level over 1m4f at the Curragh a fortnight later, again keeping on at the finish to finish fourth behind Queenstown. There's a good deal of stamina in her pedigree and the way she ran at the Curragh suggests that she'll be fully effective at 2m. Although she may remain vulnerable against the better types in maiden company, she'll be one to note granted a suitable test of stamina once she goes into handicaps. DERMOT WELD

## THE REVEREND

*3 b c Lope De Vega - Burning Rules (Aussie Rules)*

A full brother to Angel Power, who won a Group 2 and a Group 3 as a 3yo in 2020 for Roger Varian, The Reverend made his belated debut over 7f on heavy ground

at Newmarket in early November and he created a favourable impression as he ran out a stylish winner from the more experienced Strong Opinion, with a last-time-out winner nearly 5l away in fourth. Assistant trainer Maureen Haggas said afterwards: "The Reverend handled the ground better than some of the others but I wouldn't say he relished it; it's pretty disgusting out there. He looked well and behaved well, which was important and what I was pleased to see. It's taken some time to get him here, which you wouldn't necessarily think looking at him, but he's changed a lot over the year and has matured a lot physically and mentally." Angel Power improved in leaps and bounds once she started tackling 1m2f at three, so we can expect The Revered to be stepped up to that sort of trip sooner rather than later and he could be making his mark at Group level before too long.
WILLIAM HAGGAS

## TORITO

*4 b g Kingman - Montare (Montjeu)*

Although Torito showed a smart level of form last year, he's still relatively unexposed after just five outings and he's capable of making his mark in Group company this season. His season was restricted to four starts and he wasn't seen in public after Royal Ascot but, after beating two rivals in a novice at Nottingham on his reappearance in April, this one-time Derby entry stepped up a fair way when second at Sandown the following month and he turned in his best effort when beating subsequent dual winner Silver Sword (who also makes it into the "100") in a handicap at Epsom on Derby Day. Judging by the manner of that victory, he looked an interesting runner in the Group 3 Hampton Court Stakes at Royal Ascot but, although he looked a threat in the straight, his effort petered out close home and he had to settle for fourth behind Waipiro. That ended up being it for the season, though it seems

significant that he was gelded in December. He's just the type to progress again for his excellent yard and he can make amends in Group company at around 1m2f.
JOHN & THADY GOSDEN

## VANDEEK

*3 gr c - Havana Grey - Mosa Mine (Exceed And Excel)*

This dual Group 1 winner at two heads the ante-post markets for the Commonwealth Cup at Royal Ascot in June and that status is well deserved, especially as his trainer has already committed him to a sprinting campaign in 2024. It all started back in July at Nottingham where he was well supported to make a winning debut despite facing strong opposition, notably the Sir Michael Stoute-trained Never So Brave, who'd made a good impression when finishing second to Ancient Wisdom at Newmarket a few weeks earlier. Vandeek got the better of that rival despite missing the break and ducking left and, although the margin of victory was just under a length, he was always in command. Just thirteen days later he added the Group 2 Richmond Stakes to his CV despite the soft ground at Goodwood not appearing to suit him ideally. He already looked like a surefire Group 1 winner at that stage and he proved it a few weeks later when winning the Prix Morny at Deauville, in which he was able to get the better of Ramatuelle, who had won her previous three starts, two of them Group races, by upwards of four lengths. That race was also run on soft ground but he appeared to improve for faster conditions when hosing up in the Group 1 Middle Park Stakes at Newmarket, the margin of victory two-and-a-quarter lengths from the hitherto unbeaten Task Force with another solid yardstick for the grade, River Tiber, another neck away in third. His rider James Doyle was purring afterwards: "Vandeek's a pure ball of speed. He didn't jump from the gate that quick but he travelled super strong and the moment the gap opened, he put it to bed quickly. He's an electric horse and he coped with the quicker ground well, which opens up all kinds of options. I think he's a sprinter and he gave me a serious buzz there. Not many horses in a Middle Park go down to the Dip travelling as well as he did. There's a lot to look forward to." SIMON & ED CRISFORD

## WONDER LEGEND (IRE)

*4 b g Sea The Stars - Sea Of Wonders (Fastnet Rock)*

A 220,000euro breeze-up purchase in May 2022, Wonder Legend won his third career start over an extended 1m at Wolverhampton in April last year, beating Mr Buster, who would royally frank the form a few weeks later by winning a handicap by seven and a half lengths. Awarded an initial mark of 81, he made light of it a few weeks later over 1m2f at Doncaster as he ran out a 5l winner from the Alan King-trained Westerton, who would also win a handicap by a wide margin two starts later. He was punished to the tune of 13lb by the handicapper for that win but he ran another good race in the King George V Stakes over 1m4f at Royal Ascot, finishing eighth of the nineteen runners behind Desert Hero despite not being suited by the fast ground he encountered and losing a shoe. Additionally, he raced up with an unrealistically fast pace and then was hampered and carried right by a rival in the closing stages so he did exceptionally well to finish within seven and a half lengths of the winner. His final run of the year came over 1m2f at Chelmsford in August, where he failed to get involved despite being well supported and he perhaps gave notice that he was already in need of a stiffer test. Now rated 93 and gelded since his last run, there looks to be a decent middle-distance handicap in him in 2024 - a race like the Duke Of Edinburgh handicap over 1m4f at Royal Ascot looks like a viable target for him and there will be plenty of other decent

opportunities for him over that sort of trip throughout the summer, provided the ground isn't too quick.
JAMES FERGUSON

## YLANG YLANG

*3 b f Frankel - Shambolic (Shamardal)*

With a 1,500,000gns price-tag as a foal there was a fair amount of pressure on Ylang Ylang to deliver on the racetrack as she made her debut in late June and thankfully she didn't disappoint as she made all in a 7f Curragh maiden to win by a cosy two and three quarter lengths. A month later she won a Group 3 over the same trip in similar fashion, beating subsequent Group 2 winner Vespertilio by a length and a half. So far so good. However, she then came unstuck in the Group 1 Moyglare Stud Stakes back at the Curragh in September, finishing last of the nine runners behind Fallen Angel, having been headed with less than 2f to go and then eased by Ryan Moore once her chance had gone. Perhaps the quicker ground was to blame plus she raced a bit keenly in front but she was now on a bit of a recovery mission. She was ridden differently in the Group 2 Rockfel Stakes, also over 7f, later that same month, being held up in rear before coming through well late on, eventually finishing third behind Carla's Way and Shuwari. That race was again run on fast ground and the Raceform race reader said afterwards: "slightly easier ground over a longer trip is likely to see her to maximum effect" and he nominated the Fillies' Mile as an ideal next race for her. That assessment proved spot-on as she won that Group 1 contest a fortnight later, relishing the soft underfoot conditions to outstay Shuwari, who'd finished two and a half lengths in front of her in the Rockfel, by half a length. Clearly a bit of give underfoot is important to her so she may only take her chance in the 1,000 Guineas should conditions be suitable, but she looks more of a middle-distance prospect in any case and the Oaks may well prove to be the ideal race for her. AIDAN O'BRIEN

# INDEX

# 100 WINNERS
## JUMPERS TO FOLLOW
## 2024-25

Companion volume to *100 Winners: Horses to Follow - Flat*, this book discusses the past performances and future prospects of 100 horses, selected by Raceform's expert race-readers, that are likely to perform well in the 2024-25 jumps season. To order post the coupon to the address below or order online from **www.racingpost.com/shop**

Tel 01933 304858

## ORDER FORM

Please send me a copy of **100 WINNERS: JUMPERS TO FOLLOW 2024-25** as soon as it is published. I enclose a cheque made payable to Pitch Publishing Ltd for **£7.99** (inc p&p)

Name (block capitals) ........................................................

Address .............................................................................

............................................................................................

Postcode ...........................................................................

SEND TO: PITCH PUBLISHING,

SANDERS ROAD, WELLINGBOROUGH, NORTHANTS NN8 4BX